Meet Me

at the Cross

VOLUME 3

"Nations at a Crossroads"

Thanks for allowing God to use you in my life. There would be NO books w/out you bro.

RANDY CONWAY

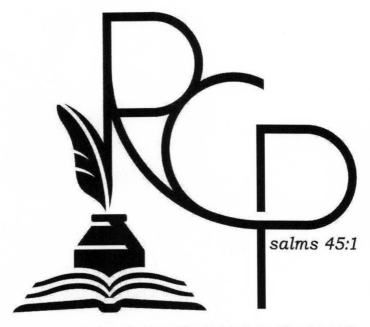

salms 45:1

RANDY CONWAY POEMS

"Truth to Empower the Soul"

Books by Randy Conway

Before Thunder Sounds Series

Before the Thunder Sounds
"Poems to Empower the Soul"
Volume 1

Before the Thunder Sounds
"Poems to Empower the Soul"
Volume 2

****

Meet Me at the Cross Series

Meet Me at the Cross
Volume 1
"The Journey to the Cross"

Meet Me at the Cross
Volume 2
"Taking Up the Cross"

Meet Me at the Cross
Volume 3
"Nations at a Crossroads"

Randy Conway's books can be purchased at:

Amazon.com

Search: Randy Conway Poems

Randy Conway Poems

Published by
Randy Conway Poems, llc
Copyright © Randy Conway, 2020

ISBN-13: ISBN: 978-0-578-64970-2

Scripture taken from the Modern English Version.
Copyright © 2014 by Military Bible Association.
Used by Permission. All rights reserved.

Cover design by

Jeffrey Mardis

Printed in the United States of America

PUBLISHER'S NOTE:
While the author has made every effort to provide accurate telephone numbers, Internet addresses and other contact information at the time of publication, neither the publisher nor the author assumes any responsibility for errors, or for changes that occur after publication. Further, publisher does not have any control over and does not assume any responsibility for author or third-party Web sites or their content.

Randy Conway Poems

website
Randyconwaypoems.com

Contact Randy Conway for speaking

engagements at:

Email: **Randyconwaypoems@gmail.com**

Find Randy at

Facebook: Randy Conway Poems
Youtube: Randy Conway Poems

Purchase paperback books and ebooks at

Amazon.com

RANDY CONWAY BIOGRAPHY

Randy Conway's poetic works have been praised by international Christian authors and researchers including Stephen Quayle, Thomas Horn, Derek Gilbert, Joe Horn, Dr. Michael Lake, Donna Howell, Wes and Justen Faull, and many more.

Conway is a loving husband of his wife Robin, for forty-six years, a father of three, and grandfather to fourteen. He loves to water ski, play piano, study Bible history, and he is an American history enthusiast. Randy is also a builder, a visionary, and a prolific poet.

One of his favorite things to do is share his poetry creatively during public speaking engagements using a multi-media presentation that includes emotionally moving music, thought-provoking visuals, and Randy's entertaining recitation of his work.

ENDORSEMENTS

"Randy Conway's poems are both a battle cry and an encouragement; forged by his unrelenting passion for the truth."
Justen Faull
Faull Brothers Productions, Fourth Watch Films

"The writing of Randy Conway combines timely warnings for our nation, with equal amounts of encouragement and hope. Prepare to be both jarred and uplifted as you read through Volume 3 of Conway's outstanding 'Meet Me At The Cross' series."
Darrin Geisinger
"Best-selling Author/illustrator – "Zero-Gs"

"Meet Me at the Cross" is an immense collection of provocative documentaries in poetic form. Randy Conway does it again!"
Wes Faull
Faull Brothers Productions, Fourth Watch Films

ACKNOWLEDGEMENTS

Once again I have to begin by giving thanks to God for the life he has given me. Believing people who encourage us daily surround Robin and me. In this third edition of *Meet Me at the Cross, Volume 3, Nation's at a Crossroad*, I hope you take time to read and ponder what it means to people as a nation to stand at the crossroads of history where we now find ourselves and choose freedom or slavery, to remain in Babylon or "to come out of her". The Bible is clear as to where and how liberty is obtained and maintained, liberty is found only in the person of Jesus Christ and He is found individually by each of us at the cross.

There have been so many people in my life, including my Mother, my Dad and my wife who have supported me through thick and thin before, during and after my salvation. My wife, Robin continues to be the brightest Christian influence in my life and I have to thank her again and again for helping me with our book series. She reads every word and checks every line. Her attention to detail is remarkable.

Thanks to all those who have seen value in my work and encouraged me along the way. Without the encouragement of those who God has put in my life, especially those ministers and researchers that God has blessed me to meet, this book would not be possible.

FORWARD
by

Michael K. Lake, Th.D.

Poetry is one of the most unique forms of human expression. It was the modern poet, Roger Housden that shared his insights regarding the power of poetry:

> *Poetry is a concise and elemental means of expressing the deepest of human emotions: joy, sorrow, grief, hope, love, and longing. It connects us as a people and a community; it speaks for us in a way few other forms of writing can do.* [1]

Housden did not stop there; he linked the need for poetry in the darkest of times. Housden continues:

> *Poetry not only matters, it is profoundly necessary; especially in times of darkness and difficulty, both personal and collective.* [2]

Historically, poetry can quickly capture the attention of the reader and serve as a way of compressing truth, emotions, and concepts into the canvas of the human mind in profound ways. The ancient Hebrews knew the power of poetry and used it to express divine truth that became a part of holy writ.

Is it any wonder that the Holy Spirit is using poetry to capture the attention of this generation and prepare them for the darkest times in all of human history? The modern Evangelical movement has all but abandoned the study of biblical prophecy. Yet, there are more scriptures that detail end-time events and the return of Christ than those regarding His first appearing. We have a younger generation that is asleep at the wheel, as prophecy unfolds.

One of the most intriguing and (for me) endearing aspects of God is that He will prepare and anoint servants that are ordinary people to do extraordinary things for the Kingdom. Who would have thought that a man, who is a contractor by trade, would be inspired by the Holy Spirit to write poems expressing biblical truth regarding the last days, while tearing back the secretive veil of the Luciferian Elite?

The poems of Randy Conway serve as spiritual caffeine to awaken the slumbering saints, as well as moving activated members of the Remnant into deeper contemplation of both the times in which they live and their Kingdom assignments. Randy can express biblical and prophetic truth in the condensed medium of poetry in ways that hours of teaching cannot. As you read through these Holy Spirit inspired sonnets, be prepared for a deep stirring in your soul. There will be times that you will be brought to tears. At other times, a fresh determination to be a faithful watchman will be released by the Spirit of Truth.

May the Holy Spirit use this collection of writings to awaken and prepare you to be used by God, as we race headlong into both the rise of the Son of Perdition and the return of the King of Glory!

Michael K. Lake, Th.D.
drlake@biblical-life.net
Biblical Life

Dr. Michael K. Lake, Th.D.
Resources and contacts

"Deep Waters to Nurture and Empower the Remnant."
TM

P.O. Box 160 | Seymour, MO 65746-0160 | USA
Phone: 417-935-2664 | Fax: 888-958-3564

College & Seminary Website: **www.biblical-life.com**
Resources: **http://store.biblical-life.com**
Assembly: **http://www.biblicallifeassembly.org**
Kingdom Intelligence Briefing:
http://www.kingdomintelligencebriefing.com
YouTube Channel:
http://www.youtube.com/biblicallife

INTRODUCTION

Freedom:

Over the course of human history freedom has been elusive to many, fought for by millions, and squandered by multiple selfish generations. Regardless of the position on the timeline of human history and irrespective of the delineation between spiritual freedom, corporate social freedoms, and personal freedom, the currency acceptable to purchase freedom has remained a constant. The currency employed in the payment for the price of freedom is and always has been blood.

The blood of the Son of God was the ultimate payment for all freedom. Any freedom outside of the liberty the cross provides is temporary and weak. Such freedom is often nothing more than bondage wearing the guise of freedom. The blood of martyrs mixes in the soil with the blood of fallen soldiers and cries out from the ground "payment for freedom." It matters not if war was waged for financial profit or for political expediency, those who engaged in the battles throughout American history have done so with a personal belief that the engagement was to obtain or to defend freedom.

If the war in which they died was not fought for the purpose of defending or obtaining freedom, then those who manipulate the waging of war for other reasons will someday be held accountable for the blood of all who were engaged. The young men and women who have committed their lives, futures and personal wellbeing have not done so for political or financial agendas. They have done so for the sake of freedom. Polycarp, who is said to have been the first follower of Christ to be martyred, died for the freedom he had found in Christ and refused to relinquish. Turn on the evening news and listen for the name of the latest American soldier to be wounded or killed in current foreign conflict, or visit the Voice of the Martyrs website and read of the latest pastor killed for his faith ... all paid the price in the required currency for freedom.

John Quincy Adams, the sixth President of the United States, said, "Posterity-you will never know how much it has cost my generation to preserve your freedom. I hope you will make good use of it." Sadly, we must confess we have not. We have squandered our liberty in this nation and we have made a mockery of the blood spilled at the foot of a cross just outside of Jerusalem over 2000 years ago. Like the puppeteers of politics and wars, will we not be held accountable for our actions as a nation?

Hasn't the Church of today by its **silence** of the **Truth** squandered and mocked what has been purchased for us in blood? Its continued cowardice and partnership with an illuminist, power-hungry, anti-Christ, Babylonian political agenda is a continuation of the squandering of our freedom and it is a dishonor to those whose blood currency has been spent.

As I ponder the loss of freedoms we have known in this country: the loss of personal identity replaced with a fiction or straw man, the loss of our Constitution, the loss of the Bill of Rights, (now nothing more than privileges meted out as TPTB see fit) the loss of the right to life for the unborn, the loss of the God ordained family, the loss of land ownership, the loss of a righteous court system, the loss of TRUTH—the list is long and disturbing—I must ask how can we regain what we have lost? Sadly, I know the answer it will require blood. Are you willing to give your life to secure what has been lost? Are you willing to sacrifice the life of your son or daughter, husband or wife to stop this spiral into a New World Order, which is an order of death and not life, an order of bondage and not freedom?

How many will be among the number of those referred to in Revelation 12:11, who "overcame him by the blood of the Lamb and the word of their testimony, and loved not their lives unto the death?"

This begs another question, how many will be among those who would rather stand upon the words of Crowley? He said, "Do as thou wilt shall be the whole of the law."

There is a way to avoid the spilling of more blood. The way is the way of repentance; the blood of Jesus is more than enough— but our repentance is required. The blood payment has been made! However, our refusal to repent prevents the payment from being applied.

Again I quote John Quincy Adams speaking to the delegates of the Thirteen Colonies on July 1, 1776, "Before God, I believe the hour has come. My judgment approves this measure, and my whole heart is in it. All that I have, and all that I am, and all that I hope in this life, I am now ready here to stake upon it. And leave off as I began, that live or die, survive or perish, I am for the declaration. It is my living sentiment, and by the blessing of God it shall be my dying sentiment. Independence now, and independence forever!"

Standing for an ideal as grand as the Declaration of Independence and this nation is a noble cause but we live in a day when that stand is insufficient. We must have men and women who will stand for the Living God and who will love not their lives unto death for the cause of Christ, who are dedicated to Kingdom living rather than Babylonian submission.

We are living in the last days when the only cause men will stand for is a cause for themselves, for men have become "... lovers of themselves, lovers of money, boastful, proud, blasphemers, disobedient to parents, unthankful, unholy, without natural affection, trucebreakers, slanderers, unrestrained, fierce despisers of those who are good, traitors, reckless, conceited, lovers of pleasure more than lovers of God, having a form of godliness, but denying its power."

(2 Timothy 3:2-5)

All of mankind, not just nations, now stands at the crossroads of time; we are looking in real time at the last days and we must choose which road we will take.

TABLE OF CONTENTS

CHAPTER 1
Regarding America

CHAPTER 2

Abortion

CHAPTER 3

When I Saw the Cross

CHAPTER ONE

REGARDING AMERICA
(The United States—how has it responded to the cross?)

AMARUCA, AMARUCA

Amaruca, Amaruca what gods do dwell in thee?

Is Behemoth in the land; is Leviathan under your seas?

Do men seek to contact the seraphs veiled in plumes?

Have we rendezvoused with the Nachash in darkened,

hidden rooms?

Do secret societies seek council with the Amaru?

Is the Bohemian Grove a part of the coming apocalyptic

milieu?

Do Quetzalcoatl and Kukulkan have offspring they are

hiding?

Are they under the ice just waiting and their time they

are biding?

Do you know how large their offspring will become?

Theirs will be a violent rule when the world becomes as one.

Atlantis may not be what the Baconians have imagined.

Can we stand against the hybrids that were made the former legends?

Was "The Babalon Working" more than just some occult ceremony?

Was a gateway opened? Is there any to give true testimony?

How long have the gates been open and how often have the gates been used?

What of the Collider? There are stories that something there has passed through.

What will transpire when the Ley Lines once again cover all the earth?

Could there be a nefarious Ley Line link behind the touted 5g Network?

What will be awakened, which for centuries has been lying silently in stasis?
Could this be the plan by those who seek control and believe they have superior gnosis?

Amaruca, Amaruca what horrible secrets now hide in thee?
We're calling evil good and good evil from sea to shining sea.
Many won't recognize by name the ancient gods revealed herein,
But they're still here—the fallen ones—and the cause for the state we're in.
There's an ancient race of hybrids and only the names have changed.
They're still working the old plan-the human DNA to rearrange.
The Artilects of tomorrow are the hybrids of yesterday;
The Cosmists, the Terrans and the Cyborgists; which will have their way?

Is Cellular Automita coming? Will we have new
artificial brains?
Will tomorrow bring Chimeras; will our DNA become
a corrupted strain?
Will Neuro Implants change us until finally humans
are obsolete?
Will a post-human society be the days of Noah and of
history a repeat?

As it was in the days of Noah so shall it be in the end
When portals were opened and all species the fallen
ones did blend.
Alien revelations and megalithic discoveries
uncovering ancient religions;
The religions of the Fallen Ones bringing soon the
Man of Perdition.

Transhuman revelations or ancient discovery, the
result is just the same;
As it was in the days of Noah, the seed of all man was
stained.

Who will prevail in a world of war when chosen
humans are enhanced?
Will those who refuse to be changed even stand a
chance?

Opening portals is still sought; opening a vial also will
suffice,
But in order to become as gods it will cost a heavy
price.
Eternal life is offered free to those who will accept
God's Son,
But those seeking immortality will find they are
undone.

Once the portals are opened, can they again be
closed?
Once germline technologies are employed, it is too
late to say no?
You cannot put a genie back in its bottle once it has
been released,

And the agenda of the watchers will bring to us
Revelation's Beast.

Keep watch with expectation that you are not
deceived.
Your consciousness should belong to God not just
another "sleeve."
There is coming a day of the Lord that all men of
earth will see,
And with His sword He shall slay the Dragon that is in
the sea.

Men will cry for death, but death will refuse to come.
Will this be the result when post human we have
become?
There is a way that seems right to men, but the end
of it is destruction;
All I have revealed herein is Eden's repeated
seduction.

Jesus stands at the door and knocks, longing to come in.

Salvation waits for the repentant, those who turn to Him.

The time grows short with each passing day; soon you will have to make a choice.

It is time to seek the Truth and be careful who you listen to; you must discern each voice.

Amaruca—Means Land of the Plumed Serpent. The Plumed Serpent is an ancient Mesoamerican god. According to Freemason Manly P. Hall, this is the actual origin of the name of the Americas.
Nachash—The Shining One, Deceiver or Diviner of Knowledge; The creature that seduced Eve in Eden.
Amaru—Peruvian name for the Plumed Serpent god.
Quetzalcoatl—The Serpent god's name as given him in Mexico.
Kukulkan—The same god as identified in the Mayan language.
The Babalon Working—An occult ritual performed by Jet Propulsion Laboratory scientist and Scientology founder, L. Ron Hubbard, in an effort to open a portal or doorway for the goddess Babalon to enter.
Artilects—A new species of man according to author Hugo De Garis in his book "The Artilect War."

The Cosmists, the Terrans and the Cyborgists—The divisions of future humanity that will ultimately clash in the final World War according to Hugo De Garis.
Cellular Automita—The form of infrastructure for artificial brains.
Transhuman—Refers to augmented or altered humans, whether by altering of the DNA or enhancement by technologies; perhaps future Chimeras.

AMERICA THE BEAUTIFUL

America, we used to be known as the land of the free
and the home of the brave;
We now exist in danger of the brave being dead and the
free becoming slaves.
An inspired composer once wrote of beautiful and
"spacious skies;"
Now poisonous clouds drift where the eagle flies.

We were the breadbasket of the world with "amber
waves of grain;"
Now the crops are tainted and the farmer's land is gone
through Imminent Domain.
The purple mountains still have their majesty, but is
there any fruit left in the plain?
Those who poison the skies and alter the seed also
withhold the rain.

"The thoroughfare of freedom" has become overgrown
with lies;
Will God crown our little good when His patience we
have tried?
It is time to remember the rest of the song, the part that
is a prayer
That we would exercise "self-control and God our flaws
repair."

We have been robbed of that which the "proven heroes bought"
By those who do not know that "gain is divine," as evil they have wrought.
I don't think it was the "patriot's dream" to establish a New World Order,
Or to establish a country without prayer, without God, or without borders.

Are there noble men that dwell within the halls of government?
Has selfish gain stained our souls to the loss of any covenant?
The "shine" upon the seas is not glimmer but disease,
And we turn our backs on God's grace so our lusts we may appease.

The words to a song penned to describe a once great nation,
But to sing America the Beautiful now brings me tears and frustration.
To know we have the promise of blessing, but men choose rather damnation,
    We have abandoned the Truth and torn down the
    early foundations.

We now will see what we have birthed for past is the
period of gestation.
The time has come for men to repent for there is
born an aberration;
It is the offspring of our sin and when full-grown
brings decimation.
America will only be beautiful again when God
receives first our repentance, then our adjuration.

*"America the Beautiful" is an American patriotic song.
The lyrics were written by Katharine Lee Bates, and
church organist and choirmaster, Samuel A. Ward, at
Grace Episcopal Church in Newark, New Jersey,
composed the music. The two never met.*
*Bates originally wrote the words as a poem, "Pikes
Peak," first published in the Fourth of July edition of the
church periodical, The Congregationalist, in 1895. At that
time the poem was titled "America" for publication.
Ward had originally written the music, "Materna", for
the hymn, "O Mother dear, Jerusalem", in 1882, though
it was not first published until 1892. Ward's music
combined with the Bates poem was first published in
1910 and titled America the Beautiful. The song is one of
the most popular of the many U.S. patriotic songs.*

(Quoted from Wikipedia free Encyclopedia)

ANYTHING

We are now in the season of anything.

Just exactly what does that mean?

The winds of war are blowing with gale force

And ANYTHING can be the catalyst to

set WW3 on its course.

The economy is a roller coaster out of control

And ANYTHING can be the event that puts us in a hole.

Civil unrest appears in every news report

And ANYTHING will spark a fire of no resort.

Political correctness has become a mindset of insanity

And ANYTHING could happen to

completely lose our humanity.

Treason is suspected of countless holders

of political office

And ANYTHING can now aggravate our losses.

The plan to reduce the world's population is advancing
And ANYTHING could move us to the killings,
not mere ranting.
Socialism and communism just won't go away
And ANYTHING could find one of them here to stay.

The weather wars keep being attributed to conspiracy,
But ANYTHING at any moment will
bring it into your reality.
The total control of humanities' masses
is rarely believed,
But ANYTHING—perhaps 5g—
will prove it to be achieved.

Vaccinations, we're told, are provided
only for our wellbeing,
But ANYTHING can be the tragedy
that proves we were unseeing.
Censorship is rampant and out of control
And ANYTHING will implement censorship patrols.

I could go on and on with every issue

facing us at every measure

And ANYTHING at all could be the event that

changes our world forever.

Perhaps that event has already taken place

and we will discover

The world that we once knew

will never be able to recover.

We are now in the season of ANYTHING;

There are no morals or values to which we cling.

ANYTHING is the season in which we now live;

At every turn we are one second away and there is

no more time to give.

ARE WE A NATION?

Are we a nation poised for destruction

Or a nation poised for instruction?

Are we a nation expecting an awakening

Or a nation looking for a darkening?

Are we a nation poised for receiving,

Or a nation poised for deceiving?

Are we a nation whose God is the Lord?

Are we a nation who is Babylon's whore?

Can we remain a nation?

"Blessed is the nation whose God is the LORD; and the people whom he hath chosen for his own inheritance." (Psalm 33:12)

B.E.A.S.T.

The Bible says that the spirit of Anti-Christ for some time
has been at work amongst us,
But who is this Beast that the people will worship, the
one in whom the world will trust?
We will know the "Man of Sin," the Scriptures say he will
be revealed,
But what of this mysterious second "Beast," and the
power he will wield?

Then there is the image of the beast that all will be
forced to bow before;
This image is given breath and speaks—a likeness of the
one wounded by the sword.
Just perhaps could it be a **B**io **E**ntity **A**nd **S**ingularity
Technology,
The ultimate A.I., not some imagined statue of
mythology?

The B.E.A.S.T. will itself control the entire world through
the Internet
And none will buy or sell or escape the vastness of his
dragnet.
He will never need to sleep and never need to eat and
never be susceptible to disease.
There will be no knowledge unknown to him—nothing he
won't hear and nothing he cannot see.

Are we preparing the way today for the coming of the two beasts?
Are we developing the technology and will scientists become the image's prophets and his priests?
From "Alexa", "Echo" and "Sophia" will this image be such a leap?
And the words of Scripture remain unread and the people remain asleep.

As long as we have the things we want the sheeple remain unstirred
And the warnings of the watchmen are spoken to the air and remain unheard.
As long as we have the things we want the sheeple disregard the cost
Until the day eventually arrives and what we once had is lost.

The image called the B.E.A.S.T. will by his power control every aspect of our lives.
He will decide who lives and dies, who will suffer and who will thrive.
Could this be the rise of the machine the Bible calls the image of the beast?
Will you bow down to the image or will you be invited to the coming marriage feast?

Time is an unknown factor and we are not privileged to know the hour of the Lord's return,
But the hour is upon us that the condition of your soul should be your greatest concern.

Your name must be written in the Lamb's Book of Life or you will not survive.
Those who choose Jesus Christ will live; those who serve the image of the Beast will die.

Revelation 13: 1-18

BIZARRO WORLD

The weather is churning like a pot too hot and boiling over;
Nations around the world right now are preparing their soldiers.
Did not Antifa say that on November 4th it all begins?
And the pedophiles are being revealed much to their chagrin.

Evil is afoot and moving through the land; time is now grown short.
For news one must now diligently search to find a true report.
What was planned and for whom back on November fourth?
What catastrophe yet will be released, what entities will come forth?

In the oceans life is dwindling; what will happen if the oceans die?
Are the insects suffering for what is happening in the sky?
The Black Plague has been reborn. Will it spread worldwide?
Why are there no more reports of Fukushima and what rides in upon the tide?

Can the good be discerned from the evil and who can
be trusted?
Have witches shined their brooms and their magic
wands been dusted?
What can we make of a world that has become in a
word, Bizarro?
Will we survive the night? Will we see tomorrow?

Scientists are curiously watching for a massive
volcano to blow;
History is being hidden so that truth the young will
never know.
Perhaps the electric grid will fail and we will live in
the dark,
And every day someone finds another possibility for
"the mark."

Who has the biggest bomb and who will send the
first missiles into flight?
When war comes to the entire world, what will be
the reason for the fight?
Slowly we had seen racial healing until a small evil
cadre brought racism back to life.
Every kind of perversion has become rampant and
has escalated to new heights.

Speaking of heights...are the "high places" still
utilized; are they still revered?
Is there something going on that the men of earth
should fear?
Are there beings under the earth, under the ice or
watching us from space?
The faults of earth are as precarious as the boiling
magma and we could see a quake.

Is it possible for man to produce a child with a robot
bride?
Can the coasts survive a giant tsunami tide?
Mars seems to be at the center of the space race
curiosity;
I'm not sure where we're heading, but we're
traveling with great velocity.

Do saboteurs of a shadow government control these
events?
What plans have been initiated? Who signed the
malevolent binding covenants?
Should we be concerned about our food and our
water?
Are there men who are destined to be slaughtered?

Pharmaceutical dependence, bio weapons and the
constant threat of war,
An economic collapse, a government coupe and
creepy portal doors,
And if this is not enough we have to find a safe cover
from the threat of falling stars.
What is a man to make of things so chaotic and
bizarre?

If you're not acquainted with the Word of God, then
you will have no answers;
You are left to think the minds of men have been
destroyed by some brain-eating cancer.
Those who know the Truth know chaos is not the
seed for birthing order.
We have simply past a time foretold; we have
crossed a prophetic border.

Do not fear the days ahead and the events yet to be
seen;
Prepare your heart, your soul and mind by getting to
your knees.
Repent and prepare today for things will continue
down this path;
There will be days of sorrow, a coming judgment
called the Day of Wrath.

The signs and warnings are a call to repentance not a call to fear.
The chaos is disturbing, but those with ears will hear
The sound of the trumpet that will call home the remnant,
And we will be caught up with Christ and leave this earthly tenement.

No man knows that day and no man knows that hour,
And we tend to forget the Bible says before that day this earth will become quite dour.
So while we're listening for that trumpet, we need to also see
All the signs that He provides and all of God's Word we need to read.

There is no escaping what Jesus said about "when you see these things."
He said our redemption is getting closer, not that it's time to leave.
Paul described to Timothy how men would act in what he called the last days;
We are seeing his words come to pass and it is time to pray.

Pray that we will be found worthy to escape rather than be enslaved.

Pray that many will repent; there are many more who will yet be saved.

Pray that we will have wisdom and be spiritually discerning.

Pray that we are not deceived and we're found ready for His returning.

"Take heed to yourselves, lest your hearts become burdened by excessiveness and drunkenness and anxieties of life, and that Day comes on you unexpectedly. For as a snare it will come on all those who dwell on the face of the earth. Therefore watch always and pray that you may escape all these things that will happen and stand before the Son of Man."
(Luke 21: 34-36)

CAN ANYONE TELL ME WHERE AMERICA HAS GONE?

Can anyone tell me where America has gone?

I can't seem to find her. Has she gone away?

Can anyone tell me where America has gone?

All that was familiar seems now so far away.

I remember learning of integrity and courage;

I remember men of honor held in high esteem.

I remember when hard work and ethics flourished;

I remember when the unsightly was kept unseen.

Can anyone tell me where America has gone?

I can't seem to find her. She is now

a long forgotten song.

I thought our government was established

for the people;

Now it seems the government is elite and

we are but the "sheeple."

We used to spy on our enemies,

those we saw as a threat;

Now we spy on our citizens and we discard our vets.

Can anyone tell me where America has gone?

Are there any left who for righteousness still long?

The New World Order is now the America of today;

The patriots are becoming weary, worn and frayed.

The Black Robe Regiments are but stories of yesterday,

And the pulpits are devoid of truth

and men no longer pray

To the one true God of all creation;

We prefer to pander to our own sensations.

And America is no longer one nation under God;

America is the habitation of lies and the home of fraud.

Can anyone tell me where America has gone?

Thank God for the watchmen

who have warned for so long.

I pray these servants have the support and

prayers of the remnant,

Because the demise of our way of life

is now dangerously imminent.

"When the righteous are in authority, the people rejoice:
but when the wicked beareth rule, the people mourn."
(Proverbs 29:2)

CELEBRATING THE FOURTH OF JULY

"And the rockets' red glare," the bombs bursting in
Central Park.
World War three is ready to ignite; it just needs a
little spark.
In Orlando dead bodies lay at the Pulse and many are
devastated,
But the Axis of Evil in DC is elated for a new excuse to
have guns confiscated.

Men in uniform, but without an oath, brutalize a
sickly child;
Who are the officers of the TSA and why are they not
reviled?
"Gives proof through the night" that the nation we
once knew is not there;
This 4th of July the fireworks should be boxed and
the people should be in prayer.

A nation is lost and there is no remorse.

A legacy is gone; is there no recourse?

The "closet" has been opened and we celebrate confusion,

And all the people are satisfied with the elite illusion.

Islam marches to war against a sleeping nation

And the enemy is protected; you dare not make accusation.

Those things we as a nation once proclaimed that we "proudly hailed"

Have become the things that will now land a patriot in jail.

The land is stolen by bureaucrats and the work of our hands is lost,

And too many living on entitlements don't know what freedom cost.

The veterans weep into their wounded hands,
wondering can America survive;
While the professional politicians keep spewing out
their polished, devious lies.
The masses seem ignorant that anything is lost or
changed;
They just want a firecracker and their 15 minutes of
fame.

Let's put a steak on the grill and celebrate
Independence Day on the Fourth of July;
Don't give a thought to morality, responsibility, our
freedoms, or that America has died.

*"Perhaps we can for a time celebrate once again if we
don't fail our president, fail our children, fail our military
personnel, fail our nation, or fail our faith by failing to
pray. Only time will tell if we can restore what we have
lost."*
— *Randy Conway*

DEAD ON THE FOURTH OF JULY

Do you remember when the 4th of July was
a day of celebration?
That was before we abandoned God and now have
abandoned Him as a nation.
It used to be a day commemorating the
independence we declared,
But now the blood-bought freedoms we have known,
by lies have been ensnared.

Now the 4th of July is for me a day of remembering
that which we have lost.
Is there hope for our nation to be restored now that
the Rubicon we have crossed?
Benjamin Franklin stated we have a Republic,
and questioned if we could keep it;
The truth be told we have lost the Republic if
we are honest enough to admit it.

It is righteousness that exalts a nation,

but sin of the people is a reproach.

Our sin remains sin, even when hidden behind

the Supreme Court's black cloaks.

"When the wicked cometh, then cometh also

contempt,"

And now the 4th of July has become a day for

Christians to lament.

It has become a day of memorial, remembering

the nation that has died;

The land of the free and home of the brave has

become

the home of lies.

Isaiah says of those who reject God:

"And thorns shall come up in her palaces,"

And as we listen and follow the noise of the demons

as through the perverse they howl,

We shall as a nation become

"...an habitation of dragons, and a court for owls."

What will pulpits proclaim on Sunday when they

speak of the 4th of July?

Will they cling to political correctness and

putrid rainbow lies,

Or will they tend the flock and feed the sheep,

preaching Jesus crucified?

Our resurrection as a nation depends on

our repentance and being purified.

The fireworks no longer will commemorate

the bombs bursting in the air;

They will remind us that America surrendered

without a shot because we didn't care.

The Living God waits on us to humble ourselves

and turn to Him and pray;

We must repent both great and small,

for we are approaching God's judgment day.

"When the wicked cometh, then cometh also contempt, and with ignominy reproach."
(Proverbs 18:3)

"And thorns shall come up in her palaces, nettles and brambles in the fortresses thereof: and it shall be an habitation of dragons, and a court for owls."
(Isaiah 34:13)

FLEETING FREEDOM

"Let freedom ring" is what we sing
While we sell our freedom cheap.
The statue calls to one and all
While we're dying at her feet.

On freedom's shore she'll stand no more
Unless we cure sin's cancer;
Fall on our knees, to heaven plead,
Is America's only answer.

When on God we call we will stand tall
And be "One nation under God."
We'll expose the lies before we die,
Proving hell has had us robbed.

A pagan statue stands in New York Harbor
with a torch held in her hand,
Supposedly a welcome call to one and all
who would venture to this land.
As followers of Christ we've a torch to hold;
we are called to bear a holy light
Showing every man sin's curse is overcome
by God's power and His might.

When God's people, the ones who are
called by His Holy Name,
Will humble themselves before our Mighty God,
bringing Him our shame,
And on our knees with contrite hearts
we fervently plead and pray,
God has promised He will heal our land
and its people He will save.

Alas, no true freedom can be found in

New York's famous harbor;

As grand as the statue seems to be,

freedom requires something larger.

A Savior hung on a rugged cross high on a barren hill;

The call He gave to one and

all is sounding from there still.

It is only in the person of Jesus Christ that

liberty may be obtained;

It is only by His grace that judgment has been restrained.

Too many who died for freedom,

sadly, had to die in vain,

And are there now too few humbled to repentance

for freedom to be sustained?

"If my people, which are called by my name, shall humble
themselves, and pray, and seek my face, and turn from
their wicked ways; then will I hear from heaven, and will
forgive their sin, and will heal their land."
(2 Chronicles 7:14)

HEARTS OF STONE

Fraudulent smiles on bitter faces;

A heart of stone the flesh encases.

Icy cold eyes just reflections of within;

I envy not the lives of such cold and angry men.

Pretending all is well while

the nation revels in wickedness;

The conscience of the people is seared

and they love viciousness.

Lacking wisdom and with necks too stiff and hearts

too hard to learn,

The message of the gospel

the foolish men have spurned.

Without repentance our future was written long ago,

To become a hissing in the eyes of the nations

because to sin we choose to hold?

The extent of our grievances is too numerous to

make a comprehensive list,

But there is yet time to seek the Lord

and the enemy to resist.

However, time is fleeting and the length of our days

is not ours to choose;

We cannot afford the gamble in waiting

for there is too much to lose.

What does it profit a man to gain the whole world

and yet lose his soul?

Today is the day for men and nations to repent

Before the final bell has tolled.

"Because my people hath forgotten me, they have burned incense to vanity, and they have caused them to stumble in their ways from the ancient paths, to walk in paths, in a way not cast up; To make their land desolate, and a perpetual hissing; every one that passeth thereby shall be astonished, and wag his head."
(Jeremiah 18:15-16)

IN GOD WE TRUST

Believe in God? In God we trust?

Wicked men of worldly lust,

To claim this as our motto do we lie?

Do we believe He came to die

To save us each from ourselves—

To redeem us all from death and Hell?

We are created in and by His fashion,

But have become little men of evil passions,

And seldom in our hearts receive

The truth that we would find

If we were not so blind:

In God to trust.

"That they all may be one; as thou, Father, art in me, and I in thee, that they also may be one in us: that the world may believe that thou hast sent me."
(John 17:21)
"Thou sayest, (but they are but vain words,) I have counsel and strength for the war. Now on whom dost thou trust, that thou rebellest against me?"
(2 Kings 18:20)

IS EVERY ONE A PEDOPHILE?

Is every one in Hollywood and Washington a pedophile?
How have we come to be so wretched and so vile?
There remains nothing hallowed or sacred anymore;
The world is drunk with the wine from Babylon's whore.

From the center of this nation I look to the west
And I see a greenhouse for growing socialists.
It is no better when I look to the east;
The growth of progressivism just will not cease.

I look to the pulpits and there it seems
Too many are members of the Clergy Response Teams.
What happened to men such as Jonas Clark and James
Caldwell?
If it were not for the Black Robed Regiments, America
would have died where the soldiers fell.

It has become a repugnant stench to watch the rise of
debauchery,
And the pollution of God's instruction and our nation's
moral property.
If the Bible was still read at all and was not becoming
illegal,
We might remember the love of money is the root of
EVERY KIND of evil.

And by such desire we have pierced ourselves
through with many sorrows,
Wondering now what will be the outcome of
tomorrow.
How much more err can we survive?
How many more days with us will God strive?

I guess I should not be surprised that pedophiles are
celebrated.
After all, the babies we don't rape, we kill, and by
government the killers are compensated.
Hollywood produces the material to educate a sexual
predator,
But when they practice what is taught, the
hypocrisies fly from the news editors.

We are sick and diseased with a vile infection
And the condition is worsening without objection.
Sin has infected the minds of the people so that they
believe a lie,
And no one hears the tortured children when they
scream and cry.

It is time to reverse this trend!
It is time for these sacrifices to end!
It is time for righteousness to stand
Before all that is left is the American wasteland!

It is time to preach the gospel, not the latest meme;
It is time to stop acting as if this torture is unseen.
It is time to remember history and why men died.
It is time to rid our nation of all the Dr. Jekyll's and Mr. Hyde's.

It is time for the people of God to become the Ecclesia.
It is time to wake up and get off our preferred anesthesia.
Of course time doesn't really exist, except for the now,
And now is when we need to kill our sacred cows.

Repent and seek the face of God while He may still be found.
Weep and sigh at the sins of the people with your face to the ground.
Engage in the warfare that the Army of God is called to;
Stop only being hearers of the Word...and do.

Pray that the children may be saved.
Pray that God will reveal that which is depraved.
Pray that our nation will no longer be enslaved
By the sin that we let enter in and is taking us to our grave.

"Go through the midst of the city, through the midst of Jerusalem, and set a mark upon the foreheads of the men who sigh and groan for all the abominations that are done in its midst."
(Ezekiel 9:8)

"Be doers of the word and not hearers only, deceiving yourselves."
(James 1:22)

IS IT TOO LATE?

Have too many drunk the Kool-Aid?

Is it too late for America to be saved?

Are there any real men left who are willing to fight?

Has political correctness succeeded

in making the wrong seem right?

Do any hear the words of truth or listen

to what the watchmen say?

Are any aware of what is happening at home

or around the world today?

How many are obsessed with the triviality coming

from the Hollywood cesspool?

Are we finished as a nation

because we are a nation now of fools?

As the old men die and are no more,

The youth have no knowledge of the days of yore.

Has righteousness been diminished

with the passing of each generation?

Have we reached the point where righteousness is
gone and in its place desecration...

Desecration of the value of life; the desecration of
God's ultimate sacrifice?
Will we have elections to vote in a new King of Fools
to rule a fool's paradise?
The Kool-Aid is sweet, but has it deluded
the minds of men
So that men have no conscience and celebrate their sin?

Who mixes this deadly poison
and passes it out for all to drink?
What prompts a man to swallow this swill
so that he can no longer think?
Have too many drunk the Kool-Aid?
Is it too late for mankind to be saved?

*"For the turning away of the simple shall slay them, and
the prosperity of fools shall destroy them."
(Proverbs 1:32)*

LAWLESSNESS REIGNS SUPREME

It is no longer safe to walk the streets for
Lawlessness reigns supreme.
Political correctness is beyond reason
and has become extreme.
"My life matters," clambers through the crowds
as they scream,
And history is the only place you can still find
the "American Dream."

We have militarized our police forces
in order to foment distrust;
Then the mobs are incited to anger
and at police the mobs are thrust
By the powers that be that desire to see
this rise in discontent.
Those same powers are pulling on the fabric of society
in order to see it rent.

It is by design that we have climbed to this
precarious place,
And America is in dire peril unless our sins we face.
The moral compass of this land is lost—
it has been erased;
Without repentance the life
we now know will be replaced...

Replaced with a totalitarian society
where we live in FEMA camps,
And those who cry "my life matters"
will line up for their hand stamp.
There was a time when the men in blue
were more than "Law Enforcement;"
We called them Peace Officers
and they were therefor reinforcement.

The community called on them to serve
whenever a problem arose;

They weren't expected to make people obey,

because the law was not opposed.

However, now we need enforcement; not for me,

but only for the other guy.

No, not for me because remember

what matters most is me, myself and I.

"Not that we are sufficient of ourselves to think any thing as of ourselves; but our sufficiency is of God;"
(2 Corinthians 3:5)

"For I say, through the grace given unto me, to every man that is among you, not to think of himself more highly than he ought to think; but to think soberly, according as God hath dealt to every man the measure of faith."
(Romans 12:3)

LIFE AND DEATH; BLESSING OR CURSE
(The place we find ourselves in every election cycle)

Some would say we are standing at a crossroads and
I guess, to some extent, I see that view.
But a crossroads would say we have multiple choices
to make, and today that isn't true.
I would say we are at a fork in the road and the
choices are between but two:
One fork is wide and many will choose the wide; the
other is narrow and those who find it are few.
Every four years we choose, as a nation and as
individuals, between the paths;
We choose between God's mercy and blessing, or His
judgment's wrath.

Some would say we are on a precipice, but I would
disagree;
We have fallen off the precipice and have tumbled
away from all reality.

We have fallen off and into a deep, dark valley and
here we are in the valley of decision;
And in this valley life and death, blessing and curse
will make collision.

We will choose between
Freedom or enslavement,
Restoration or depravement.
We will choose between
The Truth or the lies,
The Living God or the All Seeing Eye.

We will choose between
An awakening or increasing darkness,
Being a place of life or the depository of the carcass
Where the corpse will stink and the mountains drip
with blood,
And sudden destruction comes sweeping in as a
flood.

We will choose between

Coming out of the valley on our knees

Or seeing our nation become a habitation of beasts.

This is a collision of darkness and light,

A separating of the wrong and the right.

Some say that their candidate is here for such a time as this,

But too many the call of the nation they have missed.

The story of Esther is not just about the Queen,

But of a **nation** who fasted and prayed so that God would be seen.

We will choose between

Democracy and hypocrisy,

Righteousness or mobocracy.

We will choose between

Purity or pornocracy;

A Republic or an Autocracy.

In the valley of decision dead babies litter the ground;

By the lies of Satan millions remain bound.

We will choose to serve the living God

Or on the church house we must write "Ichabod."

We will choose between

A great and needed awakening

Or we will choose to come under a shaking—

A shaking so intense that it will shake men's souls.

Hear the words of the prophets spoken in the ancient

Biblical scrolls.

Fallen, fallen, we have fallen into the valley and now we

must decide;

Will we remain in this state or above our mistakes to

rise?

No man can rescue us from the state we now are in;

We must repent and turn as a nation from our sin.

The people of God are called upon this day to seek God

and pray.

As a nation we have been placed upon the scales and

weighed—

Weighed in the balance and we are found wanting,

But God is waiting and for the repentant mercy is

dawning.

*"I call heaven and earth to record this day against you,
that I have set before you life and death, blessing and
cursing: therefore choose life, that both thou and thy
seed may live:"*
(Deuteronomy 30:19)

*"Fallen! Fallen! Is Babylon the Great! She has become a
dwelling place of demons, a haunt for every unclean
spirit, and a haunt for every unclean and hateful bird. For
all the nations have drunk of the wine of the wrath of her
sexual immorality, the kings of the earth have committed
adultery with her, and the merchants of the earth have
become rich through the abundance of her luxury"*
(Revelation 18: 2-3)

<u>NEVER SEEN HERETOFORE</u>

Russia's Putin has issued an ultimatum,

China stands ready to assist and aid them.

An evil spirit has entered through America's door

And we face the real threat of nuclear war.

These things can give one a terrible fright,

Haunt your dreams or keep you awake at night.

North Korea is ruled by a certifiable madman

And we are besieged daily with political flimflam.

A monster storm is wreaking havoc;

Daily human flesh is being trafficked.

Isis continues its campaign of slaughter;

With hellish perversion they want your wives and they
want your daughters.

Deutsche Bank is teetering on total collapse
While the media mafia just tries to distract.

Germany warned its people to store some food and

water

While Europe is overrun with Muslim Jihadist

marauders.

Satanic temples are coming to American schools

And a presidential candidate has publicly called the

people fools.

The truth is scoffed at and suppressed at every turn;

How many days before our Bibles will be burned?

Continually massive military drills are underway;
The wealthy elite are preparing their private hideaways.

Black lives matter, Blue lives matter, All lives matter...

It's all just slight of hand and noisy chatter.

Weather warfare and government drones,

Forty-four Afghan soldiers on our soil, their whereabouts

unknown.

The New World Order, Agenda 21 and threats coming

from Iran,

What can we do; is there hope for man?

Science is still playing with our DNA

Coming closer to the Ubermensch everyday.

In regards to the Internet, what will be the trigger trip

To bring about a total censorship?

Politicians looking to increase their personal wealth

Even if it costs the entire nation its economic health.

Washington is scandal-ridden, our leaders seek

subversion

And the people follow their leaders wallowing in perversions.

Darkness, evil and an increasing spiritual clash,
A society can be monitored by removing the use of cash.

More spying, more lying, more dying, more crying—

Men's hearts will fail for some things will be horrifying.

Earthquakes, volcanoes, floods and drought,
And a plan for the population to be culled out.

Poisonous vaccinations, Space wars, Cyber wars and Civil

war—

We are living in a time never seen heretofore.

Now if you think all of this is just poppycock,
And it matters not the time on the "doomsday clock,"

Then you bear your own responsibility,

For to you the watchman warns in futility.

Your worldview is "I don't agree and I will live for me.

The government should pay my way so I can live for free.

Martial law is just another one of those conspiracies,

And the Bible is full of myths; I find it all a mystery."

If this is you then you need not read anymore,
But if you realize this world is not like it ever was before

And if you want to know what lies yet in store,

Continue on for there is a storm just off our shores.

You can take heart for all is not doom and all is not
gloom;
Amidst the stench of this world there is a fragrance of

perfume.

It is the songs still sung by those who personally know

Jesus Christ;

There is great hope and future for those who trust Him
with their life.

Rulers have risen and fallen, they have been
defeated and they have reigned,
But a time is approaching when not just kings, but
the Kingdoms will be changed.

"And the seventh angel sounded; and there were

great voices in heaven, saying,

The kingdoms of this world are become the kingdoms

of our lord, and of his Christ;

And He shall reign..." (Revelation 11:15)

When hope seems gone and wasted seem our tears,

"I sought the LORD, and He heard me and delivered

me from all my fears."

(Psalm 34:4)

To survive the darkness and fear of the this world

there is a simple key,

"What time I am afraid, I will trust in Thee."

(Psalm 56:3)

"In God have I put my trust: I will not be afraid what man can do unto me."

(Psalm 56:11)

You cannot be a friend of God and continue living in Satan's company,

And you cannot face tomorrow unless your preparation is on your knees;

To assume tomorrow's survival without God is the ultimate vanity.

The Bible has proclaimed it from Genesis to Revelation,

Men of God have warned and preached without reservation

That time's labor pains would come—the end of time's

gestation.

While the world is obsessed with every lurid fixation,

Not seeing the darkness or realizing its own

abominations,

While Satan has been building a black and evil

confederation,

Jesus has already won the victory and Satan will face

annihilation.

Delusions to believe a lie will spread like a great

contamination

Resulting in the death of great portions of the

population.

The prophecies are being fulfilled since we are that

generation,

And the things that lie before us are beyond our

imaginations.

Repent today and accept Jesus as your Savior; it was

for you He was crucified.

He is the only way and the only Truth and He is life.

*"And when these things begin to come to pass, then
look up, and lift up your heads; for your redemption
draweth nigh."*
(Luke 21:28)

*"And it shall come to pass, that whosoever shall call
on the name of the Lord shall be delivered: for in
mount Zion and in Jerusalem shall be deliverance, as
the Lord hath said, and IN THE REMNANT WHOM
THE LORD SHALL CALL."*
(Joel 2:32)

PARADISE ABANDONED

Fear is the most obvious word to describe
Those that under their canvas tents do hide.
Fear is felt by the homeless on the streets
And fear spills over onto those whom the homeless
meet.

People are afraid of those living in the tents;
Those in the tents are afraid of unknown intent.
To live a life without a home is to live in fear;
It is indeed an untamed and frightening frontier.

The sheer volume of garbage and filth is beyond
comprehension;
In Los Angeles alone the geography of the homeless has
reached a point of distension.
Across the country and around the world the homeless
shelter in the streets,
Begging from the sidewalks and looking in the garbage
for something to eat.

Acres of humanity suffering in filth and poverty
And the numbers are growing with disconcerting
velocity.
Mental illness is rampant in this makeshift community
While drug addiction enslaves them all and the drug
lords have impunity.

Disease festers and grows, unrestricted and undeterred
Becoming a pandemic running through this human herd.
The illnesses we thought were left behind in the
medieval ages
Are breeding prolifically and no longer live only on
history's pages.

TB is exploding, along with Typhus and Black Death;
L.A. is called a petri dish for disease spreading with every
breath—
Spreading Hepatitis A, parasites, HIV, Cholera and Staff
While rodent infestations are so voracious that they
can't be graphed.

Sex offenders wander the streets looking for another victim.

Is homelessness an issue? A scourge? A problem or just a symptom?

A symptom of a society that has lost any knowledge of the value of life?

A symptom of a society where moral decay has become rife?

It is a darkness and blackness that overwhelms people and the land;

It is the absence of Light and perhaps part of an age-old plan.

A plan to reduce the population is no secret, but well known;

In fact, the plan is there for all to see etched into a stone.

In a brutal environment where disease is growing undetected,

We are one cough away from masses being affected.

It is a human weapon of mass destruction

Assisting those desiring a human reduction.

Abused people, hurting souls, abandoned people left to

die,

Addicted people, lost souls, displaced people who are

terrified,

But that is just one view of this predicament...

Some are there because they choose; to stay is their

intent.

Oh, there are efforts made for the public eye by

governments;

To study this problem, by one city 620 million dollars

was spent.

After such an amount you wouldn't think 60,000 still live

in tents;

It is hard to fathom and difficult to make sense.

I see this problem as the result of wars—wars we lost.

The displacement of too many people were the wars' costs.

They exist on the streets because we lost the war on drugs;

The war on poverty was not won and on the sidewalks runs the blood.

In the homeless camps dwells the targeted damage of our favorite social wars;

As politicians fabricate a cause, the victims multiply by the score.

They are victims, they are wounded, they are weapons, and they are dead.

For the Zombie apocalypse the homeless are the beachhead.

They are the walking dead—the unwitting zombie soldiers.

These zombies don't have to bite; you're infected by exposure.

The unfortunate stay in the streets while we cater to those crossing our border.
A difficult thing to justify, it seems to me to be quite out of order.

We have groomed generations and educated them to DO NOTHING and EXPECT CHANGE,
And those false expectations promised by deceivers have become their chains.
The homeless are in fact nothing more than pawns in a vile and dimensional game
And rather than search for solutions, the liberal voice just passes blame.

L.A. is called a "Sanctuary City"...perhaps someone should provide a definition.
Since taking on that status, what was once called paradise is turned to hell by attrition.
Wearing down the saints, wearing down the voices of reason and common sense,

Spending millions of dollars to buy another tent is
not solution...it is pretense.

Endlessly taught that life is not of great value until
life is no longer cherished,
Life without value destroys dreams and "where there
is no vision people perish."
And the progressive still teaches that only
government can be our salvation,
But until the Truth is shared, the homeless will
remain in their frustration.

In all fairness there are those who are just one
paycheck away:
They could find themselves in dire straits in the span
of just one day.
Unreasonable tax cuts assist the undocumented, but
you are the one who pays,
And the self-appointed thinking they're gods will
determine your fate.

Venezuela should be an example of how socialist systems conclude
With no housing, no wages, no welfare and no food.
But to give council to a fool is an exercise in futility
And the masses will die to ensure the elite's utopian tranquility.

Socialist's attempts at remedy end with continued misery and imminent peril,
And the homeless population increases as it continues growing feral.
With poverty overtaking and the divide between the haves and have nots spreading,
A disease-laden, stench-filled zombie pandemic is where we're heading.

The ground is quaking and the earth is shaking,
The temperature's rising until its breathtaking,
The water is falling incessantly and will not stop
And the effect is disastrous upon our crops.

If you think the homeless situation is a problem now,

Wait until we ALL need food and we're asking HOW?

When all becomes dark the danger level will
dramatically increase

And any normality of life as you have known it will
instantly cease.

This is a situation that is more than simmering—it is
now festering—

And I believe it is being manipulated and agitated for
our sequestering.

Kissinger said if you control the food you control the
hordes.

Our problems persist because we gave up our nation
and God is not our Lord.

Yes, Jesus fed the masses with some fish and with
some bread,

But Jesus has been banned and elite government
officials placed in His stead.

"Sin is a reproach to any people" is what the Scripture says,
And the end result of the homeless problem will be to count the dead.

Those areas of our country once considered paradise are gone;
They have morphed into Gehenna and the people have been conned.
Paradise Lost doesn't quite describe the carnage and desolation
Which is now the wasteland teaming with filth that has become our nation.

"Due to decades of misguided and faulty policies, homelessness is a serious problem. Over half a million people go homeless on a single night in the United States. Approximately 65 percent are found in homeless shelters, and the other 35 percent—just under 200,000— are found unsheltered on our streets (in places not intended for human habitation, such as sidewalks, parks, cars, or abandoned buildings). Homelessness almost always involves people facing desperate situations and extreme hardship. They must make choices among very limited options, often in the context of extreme duress, substance abuse disorders, untreated mental illness, or unintended consequences from well-intentioned policies. Improved policies that address the underlying causes of the problem and more effectively serve some of the most vulnerable members of society are needed."

The State of Homelessness In America
The Council of Economic Advisers
September 2019
www.Whitehouse.gov

RED OCTOBER

A Red October will not be limited to
the color of the sky;
A Red October will be a time when the mettle of men
is tried.
A Red October will be remembered for the flood of
tears that were cried;
A Red October will not be remembered for Tricks or
Treats or pumpkin pie.

A season of blood and a climate of trouble lie at the
threshold of tomorrow;
Time is in God's hands, but I believe the time left is
only borrowed.
Will men be delivered to trouble, to astonishment,
and to hissing
Because all warnings and scripture for too long we
have been dismissing?

The time is now upon us that we must stand and
dress for battle;
We have been warned, we have been commanded to
come out of Babel.
Those whose names are in the Book of Life—you're
here for such a time as this;

Beyond human comprehension are those who are coming from the abyss.

The demonic parasitic forces are at work engineering this world's conflicts;
Satan, the king of the world, waits under the ice to ready his plan to inflict.
Sadly there are churches embracing evil, practicing every kind of paganism,
And so it is that men have become a part of the enmity—a very ancient schism.

Who will be wearing red shoes this coming Halloween?
Perhaps followers of the ancient gods, those worshippers of Athene?
Will there be spirit cooking and soul cakes this all hallows eve?
Red October will be a time when for missing children mothers grieve.

Do you know your identity? Do you know who you really are?
Choices will be presented and loyalties made sure; that time is not afar.
Did not Bush Sr. give away the plans for a neutron bomb?

I don't know about you, but knowing who has it gives
me qualms.

There have been signs in the sky but sadly they have
been scoffed.
There is one who saw an ominous giant blackbird...it
is now aloft.
Written on its wings is "Power has been given unto
me;"
"I want to make war" is also written on its beak.

Higher entities will be welcomed by those who do
not know their Creator
And those they welcome will reveal themselves as
our terminators.
Those who serve the darkness do not originate from
this planet
And they are more than ready to take advantage of
the fool's enchantment.

Let those with ears hear and understand;
May the Ecclesia prepare to make a stand.
Live in, not put on, the whole armor of God.
Be not deceived; this world is ruled by fraud.

What will happen in a Red October I can't really say;
It was a bloody Revolution that coined this phrase.
Prophecy is rapidly unfolding before our very eyes
And every day another perverted evil by society is
normalized.

To find the truth turn off the agenda driven falsehoods
pretending to be news.
You will gain nothing by ignoring God and eternally
everything you will lose.
"Heaven and earth will surely pass away;" in the Word it
is so inscribed.
But God's "Word endures forever;" it is living and will
never die.

There will be great tribulation such has never been seen
before;
History has no record or any reference to describe the
coming horror.
The winds of war blow as a gale and unrest is creeping
under every door
And men entrenched in a strong delusion will not
abandon Babylon's whore.

"Come out of her my people and be not partakers of her
sins;"

You will find this command to be essential when the plagues begin.
An earthquake is coming that will cause even the remnant to be afraid;
Now is the time for us to repent and this very moment is the time to pray.

"The righteous cry, and the Lord hears and delivers them from trouble;"
Those who rise up against the Most High God will be reduced to stubble.
It is now a most critical time that all men know their true identity
Is to belong to the only One who HAS ALWAYS and WILL ALWAYS hold true SUPREMACY.

"Thou art my rock and my fortress; for Thy name's sake guide me,"
"My times are in Thy hand: deliver me from mine enemy."
Let the lying lips be put even now into silence;
As a "Warrior Class of Christian" I will not bow to compliance.

A Red October could in fact be coming now upon us—
A Red October when into a new normal we will be thrust,

A Red October when spells are cast and children
sacrificed,
A Red October when war could define a new zeitgeist.

A Red October will not just describe the color of the
autumn sky.
A Red October will determine with whom you are allied;
A Red October that calls us to uphold His righteousness,
A Red October when there is no more time for idleness.

The converging of crowns is coming at a frightening
rate—
The economic crown and the secret London banksters
will see their fate;
The military crown and the subverting DC minions will be
revealed as fakes;
The religious crown is coming down and the Vatican
City's evil potentate.

Much must transpire before we see the end,
But a Red October could be where it begins.
One day the kingdoms of this world will become the
kingdoms of our Lord
And He shall rule them with a rod of iron and the world
will feel His sword.

"And I looked, and behold a pale horse: and his name that sat on him was Death, and Hell followed with him. And power was given unto them over the fourth part of the earth, to kill with sword, and with hunger, and with death, and with the beasts of the earth." (Revelation 6:8)

Scriptures used or paraphrased in these verses: 2Chronicles 29:8, Jeremiah 18:16, Ephesians 6:11, Revelation 18:4, Esther 4:14, Luke 21:25, Matthew 24:35, Revelation 11:13, Psalms 34:17, Psalms 31:3, Psalms 31:15, Revelation 11:15

From an article in wnd.com, June 6, 2017

"A judge sentenced three Muslim refugee boys in the sexual assault of a 5-year-old girl in Idaho, but nobody knows the length or terms of the sentence because the judge has barred everyone in the courtroom, including the victim's own parents, from speaking about the case. The three boys — two from Iraq, ages 7 and 10, and one from Sudan, aged 14 — pleaded guilty in juvenile court to multiple counts of sex crimes in an incident that occurred last June in Twin Falls. The assault occurred at Fawnbrook Apartments, when 5-year-old Jayla, who is developmentally disabled, was lured into a laundry room, stripped of her clothing and sexually assaulted while the oldest boy filmed the entire incident."

ROLLING OUT THE RED CARPET
TO DESTRUCTION

They say, "A mind is a terrible thing to waste," and that indeed is a tragedy.
Innocence lost can never be regained and bears lifelong gravity.
This is a story of three little boys who had their innocence undermined,
And a little girl who had hers stolen in an egregious and heinous crime.

While at play in what was believed the safety of her apartment complex,
Not in some far off land but in Idaho, USA, she is forced to reap the effects
Of the folly of political correctness to make all believe that Islam is a religion of peace,
And at five years old she is attacked, her innocence ravaged by this religious beast.

Although the perpetrators were little boys, the mastermind was a religious ideology
Instilled in them at a tender age so they would cleave to its theology.

How could boys so young plan to commit such an evil deed?
I believe they too are victims–victims of the Islamic creed.

Now this little girl must live in constant fear along with her siblings, parents and neighbors.
How will she deal with this event as she grows? Will in her mind remain memory's sabre
Of the moment when she was robbed of safety, her childhood and innocence?
I hold that the greatest guilt belongs to those in Washington who are so insolent.

We have rolled out the red carpet with flowers and fanfare to destruction.
There is no justice in the courts, for they too are a part of this seduction
To threaten our citizens and defend the infiltration of our communities,
And for political correctness they offer to any "refugees" all immunity.

Is Idaho an isolated event or is Idaho the Index Case for a coming epidemic
Of more Islamic nurtured little boys to wreak on the infidels hell's endemic?

———

How much money changes hands to welcome falsely
named "refugees?"
For 30 pieces of silver one can buy untold treachery.

If this little Idaho girl is the primary patient of this
perverted pandemic,
Your wives, your daughters and even your sons
aren't safe from the epidemic.
The pervasive attitude in this Nation is to quell the
Gospel– which is the vaccine–
And our crumbling borders have destroyed the
opportunity for quarantine.

Conspiracy theory, bias, racism, and islamophobia
are all terms to hide the facts.
*"In a time of universal deceit, telling the truth is a
revolutionary act."
There are more victims than I have yet described in
this unsightly tale;
The remaining victims are the citizens of this country
as we welcome the horseman pale.

I pray for those enslaved by the doctrine of Islam, which is Jihad;
Jesus died for Muslims and desires to free them from their bonds.
While we must recognize the need for prayer, we must not forget
That the followers of Islam accede to Sharia, which translated in Islam means submit.

If we continue to threaten the Word of God and the voice of reason with threats of arrest,
Our children will be raped and our security stolen as common sense is suppressed.
The urine that was expelled upon a little girl's innocent frame
Will run through our streets mingled with our blood to America's shame.

How many victims will suffer for how many years for a political goal?

The guilty, without repentance, will ultimately be
sentenced to Sheol.
Is your family safe? Have you sought your own
repentance?
I would not face tomorrow without Jesus, for the
enemy is relentless.

The war is on and the battle may be coming to the
place you live.
Pray for today's victims and the peace that only Jesus
gives.
Pray for the awakening of the people of this great
land.
Pray there will be an end to vileness and a Godly
flame be fanned.

Be watchful that you are not deceived by the enemy;
He would have you face this battle without
weaponry.
Regardless of what may come tomorrow, "the
weapons of our warfare are not carnal,

But mighty through God to the pulling down of

strong holds," and these weapons are eternal.

"For the weapons of our warfare are not carnal, but mighty through God to the pulling down of strong holds;" (2 Corinthians 10:4)

- Quotation generally attributed to George Orwell

<u>SURRENDERED</u>

The America we once knew is gone and it is no more;

We have surrendered while most didn't know we were

at war.

Multifarious battles were fought over many years—

Battles hidden from our sight and often the enemy, our

peers.

Whether long fought or quickly ended the same results

were engendered;

By our silent acquiescence or distraction, America has

surrendered.

The enemies of freedom, with hellish inspiration,

remained persistent,

Ever advancing their cause and all too often without

resistance.

History has been revised, falsified, corrupted and even

deleted,

And we now live in a day when history will be repeated.
We have surrendered the truth for the comfort of lies,
An unconditional surrender and our freedom has now
died.
We have surrendered our rights that were demanded
before our Constitution would be ratified.

As long as we receive a government check that's
certified, we can lie to ourselves that it is justified.
Not so long ago a monster was released from Jekyll
Island and we surrendered our economy;
Every generation since is forced to redistribute wealth
because of the victory of traitor bankers who control our
money.

We have surrendered all hope of present or future
prosperity
And have assented to live as slaves in financial
dependency.
We have surrendered the responsibility and privilege to
be a people of Biblical literacy,

And by so doing have become a nation without integrity.

From the office of the President to the teachers in our schools,
Sexual perversion and permissiveness has made men and women wretches, whores and fools.
By surrendering both our personal and national integrity,
We have given a greater ease to our enemies who continue to garner victories.

Politicians and leaders who cannot be threatened, bought or compromised
Have continually and often mysteriously died or reportedly "committed suicide."
We have ignored our duty to throw off a government pursuing a design of absolute despotism
And have surrendered our future security to Illuminati activism.

We have surrendered our courts and constitution;

We have surrendered all sacred institutions;

We have surrendered the victories of our forefather's revolution;

We have surrendered our minds to the onslaught of intellectual pollution.

Of greatest distress and dire consequence has been the surrender of our pulpits;

Ignoring the Word of God to preach political correctness, sermons are but refuse fit only for the toilet.

The surrender of the pulpits paved the way to surrender education, entertainment and the family;

All moral high ground has been lost and what is unnatural is now accepted commonly.

We have lost our privacy, honesty and civility,

Surrendering our decency, dignity and sovereignty.

Upon the Mastery of the Human Domain we will be but detainees;

Until we fight for right and surrender only to Christ, this will be our destiny.

This timeless war has come with the shedding of much blood;
Those who've never tasted life have paid the highest price, for abortion rages as a flood.
Men who fought valiantly for freedom have been used as pawns in evil designs
And the enemy marches on battling to destroy the human bloodline.

We have surrendered the futures of those not yet grown;
They will never savor the freedoms the past generations have known.
We have surrendered our will and our minds and now live under a great delusion,
Pretending all is orderly and well while the world is in confusion.

What is left, who is left that has not or is not surrendered?

Is not the final hour upon us when the question of our guilt must be answered?

Is there still time? Are there soldiers left enough to fight?

Who will wear the armor of God and face evil in the power of His Might?

Every day around the world Christians die in torturous agony,

But as long as men die on distant shores, America will pursue meaningless activities.

Alas, those who've never realized there is a war that rages

Will very soon realize that surrender will demand its wages.

We have moved from ridiculing or ignoring the Watchmen to labeling them as psychotic;

Our surrender has had a dimensional effect transporting the chaotic.

There is no more ground that can be lost or all will be held by the despotic;

The events ahead will be prophetic—we will stand for Christ or surrender to the demonic.

What are the terms of your surrender? How will you choose to live?

All to Jesus I surrender, all to Him I freely give.

To surrender to Jesus Christ is to win this war

And will nullify the *surrenders* we've complied with heretofore.

The America I once knew is gone and it is no more;

The stench of our sin is repugnant and will not be ignored.

The instruction of Scripture is offered–we can accept it or ignore.

We will be but a memory of history or we will repent and be restored.

"I surrender all, all to Jesus I surrender, I surrender all."

"Be not deceived; God is not mocked: for whatsoever a man soweth, that shall he also reap. For he that soweth to his flesh shall of the flesh reap corruption; but he that soweth to the Spirit shall of the Spirit reap life everlasting."
(Galatians 6:7-8)

SURVIVING THE FALL

Falling, falling, falling...we have been falling for eons
now.
Who can survive the fall when we hit the ground?
The fall began in the Garden God planted in the East
And we are falling faster now and the falling has not
decreased.

How are we to survive the fall?
Is there help upon which we can call?
There are a few who will be spared;
God made a plan while we're still in the air.

Gravity is not that which pulls us to the ground;
Gravity is the condition in which we are found.
Grave conditions that lead to death;
Grave conditions by our sin beset.

Unruly, ungodly and lovers of ourselves,
Believing in false gods and into darkness we delve.
Increasing the rate at which we fall through life;
Eventually all will know the wrong and the right.

Dishonest politics that push us all deeper into the fall—
Knowledge absent of character is what it is called.
Pleasure without conscience has an ultimate
consequence,
Desiring wealth without work, but calling it
"entitlement."

Morality is lost in business and in our personal choices;
We want religion without sacrifice, giving false doctrine
voices.
In all the sciences there is no regard for humanity,
Just a pushing of the agenda of insanity.

If asked how the human race is evolving,
Some are just through the fall surviving.
Others don't even know we are falling;
They haven't read the Word or responded to the Savior's
calling.

There is much evidence of our falling,
The deeds of men becoming increasingly appalling—
None so grievous or as militant
As the agenda to destroy the innocent.

Doubters find it difficult to believe
That forbidden knowledge came from a tree,
Yet those same doubters readily receive
That some benevolent aliens fathered you and me.

God made a way when man first fell and entered into
slavery...
Slavery to sin and to the fall, and the only escape is
Calvary.
When the fall has come to its finality and our days come
to an end,
You will not survive the impact that the end of time will
send.

Ignoring the truth, men work to repair the veil that
Jesus tore in two—
A blasphemous endeavor by principalities and
powers fueled.
To build a temple to replace the one God placed
within each of us
Is to diminish the sacrifice of Jesus who rebuilt the
Temple from the cross.

"It is finished" was His cry from the battle place of
Calvary's abomination;
To make any other sacrifice is an abomination
causing desolation.
And so the falling has deluded the minds of men and
this is their fixation;
Those surviving the fall are those who know Jesus is
the only means of Salvation.

Falling, falling, falling, but one day—we know not
when—the falling will come to its end;
To survive the fall you must be counted with those
called to ascend.
We are fallen men in a fallen world, falling to the
grave,
But Jesus offers you a way that from the fall you
might be saved.

Will you survive the fall?
Will you respond to His call?
The fruit looks just as desirable today as it did in the
beginning;

Men still fall desiring forbidden knowledge and it will be
their ending.

Surviving the fall will be a remnant;
Ignoring the call, the naked continue to their detriment.
A covering of blood has been provided for all;
Only those who are covered will survive the fall.

(Genesis 3: 1-24)

THE AGE OF DECEPTION

We are living in the Age of Deception.
Can you trust the things you see?
Can you know what to believe?
Is there any truth buried beneath the lies?
Can you see it if you try?

Too many trapped because they were intrigued;
Too many dead because they were deceived.
Powers play with the minds of men,
Tripping them with dark inception,
Owning men in the Age of Deception.

Principalities in heavenly places probably are amused
Listening to the talking heads on the TV news.
No longer reporting events, but carefully molding your
point of view.
Watching lights above floating in the sky—
So many opinions, but never identified.

A way to Truth was provided and perhaps the Father
now is grieved,
For warnings were given long ago but were not received.
"Take heed" — the words spoken— "so that you won't
be deceived."
Not a philosophy to contemplate, but words spoken with
authoritative inflection.
Spoken for those who would hear, it was a prophecy of
the Age of Deception.

The Greek poet, Hesiod, attempted to identify history's ages
With Golden, Silver, Bronze, Heroic and Iron being the stages.
Mixing science with history we have added Ice, Stone, Copper and Space—
All attempting to describe the history and future of the human race.
But I say we have been living or existing only because of grace.

The turnings of generational cycles over and over again,
There is nothing new that exists under the sun—what is today has been.
Deception rightly is the name for the age in which we now exist,
For folly is accepted while the Truth man still resists.
And sleeping fools stumble blindly through the political correctness mist.

Here's a bit of history of man's earliest years:
The words of the Nachash were smooth and delicious to the ears,
As though he had been rehearsing them for years,
Like a fine wine aged to its ultimate perfection.
And Eve succumbed to them without any hesitation.

The unique beauty of his shimmering appearance made it impossible to look away,

And the same token impossible not to hear the words he
had to say.
As in the days of Eden today is no exception;
Entranced by the beauty of lies, we have no perception.
And the world is intently listening to the voices of
deception.

Are we not deceived because we are defiant?
In our pride believing our own strength can slay the
giants,
And even the elect become deceived and are companied
with the compliant.
Our pride wants us to believe that we can transfer into a
sleeve,
And great will be the fall of those who by this lie become
deceived.

Deception can be overt or it can be very subtle;
It will censor truth and deny a voice if to the lie it would
make rebuttal.
Just try and find a mainstream source that will be honest
regarding vaccinations.
Can the motive be discovered for world-wide
"immigration?"
Immigration is what it's called, but a more appropriate
term would be Invasion.

How about a genderless society? Now that one takes the
biological cake.
The results of that delusion will be devastating when it is
fully baked.

Poison food, poison air, entitled to my healthcare, and snowflakes needing teddy bears,
Medicare, welfare, solar flares, warfare and the obvious absence of prayer.
Can you manage to untangle the truth from deception ... anywhere?

The USA was once a Republic but is now a giant corporation.
Money once had value, but because of butcher bankers it is suffering ablation.
We're all enemies of the state thanks to actions taken in1913 and 1933,
But we don't care as long as we are popular on the Social Media Marquees.
And so an entire nation has become lovers of self and the masses are deceived.

If you're not convinced we are living in the Age of Deception,
Just look at DARPA, HAARP, The Patriot Act and secret FEMA installations.
Why has the UFO disclosure been replete with years of misdirection?
Are there schools of higher learning or just places of indoctrination?
Can you trust the things you see? Do you know what to believe in the Age of Deception?

I haven't touched on false religions or the new age movement–

The lie that says we're our own deity or those who fall to that inducement.
Many are the false teachers and false preachers telling lies to their recruitments.
The deception and wisdom of this world is the enemy of God without exception.
Can you trust the things you see? Do you know what you can believe in the Age of Deception?

If we were not living in the Age of Deception, Nancy Pelosi would not be an elected official and Adam Schiff would
never be a guest on the Evening News.
If we were not living in the Age of Deception, the television networks would never air programming such as The View.
If we were not living in the Age of Deception, drag queens would not be allowed to influence children in our schools.
If we were not living in the Age of Deception, the masses would not be anxiously awaiting the latest King of Misrule.
We missed the warnings of the Son of God when He told His disciples to take heed so that we would not be fooled.

The Age of Deception is proven through the cover-up of child sacrifice of the elite;
The Age of Deception is proven with the censorship of every truthful "tweet."

You cannot deny the Age of Deception when you examine all the programs hidden from our sight, Especially considering human trafficking, mind control victims and what is determined to be their plight.
If you are not yet quite convinced, then let me continue if I might.

Epstein didn't kill himself; and why has that story suddenly gone completely silent?
How can it be that dead bodies follow the Clintons like flies following dung and all the world is pliant?
The Age of Deception reveals the deceived through the actions and rhetoric of the lawless and defiant.
What about the cover-up of ancient Nephilim—the giants of the ancient myths?
The stories that have been buried along with bones by the Smithsonian would make a lengthy list.
Strange sounds, the unexplained and cataclysms growing, and in a Crisis of Truth we now exist.

Civil war is at our door because too many like the feeling of being deceived.
The Age of Deception is marked by an Era of Treason and the founding Father's must be grieved.
Christians are being persecuted and dying by the score and the world covers up their screams,
A circus parades through the Vatican as multiple volcanoes explode their ash into the air,
And Virginia has become a battleground for freedom and few there are who care.

If this were not the Age of Deception would
children's stories train them to be witches?
If this were not the Age of Deception we would know
the truth about Coronaviruses.
If this were not the Age of Deception you could not
be imprisoned for an infection in your sinuses.
If this were not the Age of Deception, there would be
no cover-up of Vitamin C and revoking Natural
Healing Doctor's Licenses.
If this were not the Age of Deception, would FEMA
be buying weapons, body bags, and guillotines?
If this were not the Age of Deception would TPTB be
building giant data collection machines?
This is the Age of Deception, so Christian, "take heed
so that you are not deceived."

The Age of Deception will be marked by attacks
against God Himself.
Others cannot see through the deception for you,
you must awaken for yourself.
The Age of Deception will be remembered as the
Generation of Lies.
When the children were being sacrificed and no one
heard their cries.
In the Age of Deception nothing is at it appears
And dark forces are continually playing on your fears.

It is a time of hiding the truth of things affecting
climate change;
It is a time when the unrighteous and those without
virtue reign;

When the sun, tectonic plates, the magma pools and magnetosphere were ignored–
An age when there has been a continual clashing of the sword.

The Age of Deception hid the truth from us even in the labeling of our food.
It is an age wherein the people are convinced to love the profane and the lewd.
History will record the Age of Deception as a time of false flags and false wars,
A time when the Soros's of this world had it all and yet they wanted more;

An Era of Treason when the righteous were continually under attack,
And the Watchmen had little help—even from their brothers—to fight back.
A time when those who expose the lies and tell the Truth are denied any public platform,
And the agenda to seize control is paramount, forcing the masses to all conform.
The Age of Deception will see the terrifying rise of the Black Awakening,
And the only Salvation for mankind will be a biblical proportioned shaking.

This Age has seen a prolific rise in false doctrines, teachings and religions;
This Age will testify to the time when we witnessed the death of altruism.

The Age of Deception is the period of self-promoting lies from the pulpits.
Those who live without fear in this new Dark Age will be God's Remnant.

The Fallen Angel and Deep State propaganda has targeted this age's generations;
Evil plans have been implemented to achieve a chemical castration.
Entertainment and even sporting events have become profane,
All in an attempt to show for God the enemy's virulent disdain.
The age whereof I speak is filled with untold government cover-ups,
And every day wrath is being poured by buckets into God's judgment cup.

We have now seen generations of silencing the truth through murder or incarceration.
We have seen generations of suffering through pharmaceutical causation.
We have seen generations of earthquakes, flood, fire, political crimes and famine.
We have seen generations of evil rising for the sake of power and for mammon.
We have seen generations being vilified for possessing an opposing opinion,
We have seen unfounded accusations calling righteousness and morality racism.

There are questions surrounding such things as the
landing on the moon,
There are questions surrounding truth while the
righteous are impugned,
There are questions why some have blackened eyes
and are wearing ankle boots,
There are questions of coming asteroids that upon
the earth will be loosed.
But there is no question as to the source of this
world's evil, its intentions or its roots.

Secret societies have flourished in the Age of
Deception
While Christian persecution we are told is just a
misconception.
The resources of both people and the world have
been raped,
And by Alexa, Siri, and Facebook our principles and
dogma have been shaped.
Have we sacrificed privacy and families for
technology, disregarding what is at stake?

The Age of Deception will be disclosed by coming
catastrophic events.
The Age of Deception will end when Truth is at last
allowed ascent.
The Age of Deception, the Era of Treason and the
Generation of Lies
Are not beyond our Father or beyond our prayers,
for He still hears our cries.

God has not relinquished His throne nor broken any of His covenants;
He will not be usurped by satanic ritual or secret societies in governments.
There remains Salvation for those repentant and those who will seek His face,
For the Age of Deception has not even nearly expired God's boundless Grace.

There remains a true and eternal hope for all who trust in Him.
There remains a sure and strong shelter for those who repent of sin.
There remains the promise of eternal life regardless of the ages of man.
There remains for His children a heavenly blueprint—God's perfect plan.

He will make for me the Age of Deception an Age of Victory.
Even if you think that might sound contradictory,
God has worked in dichotomies throughout all of history,
And His story, by His Living Word, has already revealed this age's mysteries.

"Then Jesus said to those Jews who believed Him, "If you abide in My word, you are My disciples indeed.
And you shall know the truth, and the truth shall make you free."
They answered Him, "We are Abraham's descendants, and have never been in bondage to anyone. How can You say, 'You will be made free'?"
Jesus answered them, "Most assuredly, I say to you, whoever commits sin is a slave of sin.
And a slave does not abide in the house forever, but a son abides forever.
> *Therefore if the Son makes you free, you shall be free indeed."* (John 8:31-36)

Matthew 24:4 "...Take heed that no one deceives you."

"To be deceived in the Age of Deception is to be deception's slave. To be free is to respect the warning to be awake (to "take heed") so that you are not deceived. Freedom from slavery, freedom from deception is to know the Truth."
— Randy Conway 2019

THE ANGEL IN THE WHIRLWIND

A wind is moving, swirling with ever increasing ferocity;
It is a whirlwind coming, traveling with great velocity.
Tearing at the ground and the dirt, from earth it takes flight,
Blocking out the sun until the day becomes as night.

It is a whirling desolation that brings astonishment and decay,
Yet there are men who have longed and waited for this day.
They are looking for an angel riding in the wind
And hoping to ignite a fire within the minds of men.

A fire that burns away all freedoms and leaves blackness in its place
While a wasteland is the end result left in the whirlwind's wake.
And those who call themselves enlightened believe they will share
In leading a New World Order, as they are Lucifer's heirs.

Throughout history men believed this angel was benevolent,

With secret knowledge passed through time guided by malevolence.
Even presidents in speeches referred to this mysterious whirlwind event,
Believing they are the illumined ones speaking with coded intent.

But the whirlwind they will meet is of the Lord, going forth in fury!
It falls grievously upon the wicked as they are judged most surely.
For Lucifer's minions have sown corrupted seeds into the wind
And as they reap the whirlwind it shall mark their end.

Then God's remnant will be found willing in the day of power
From the womb of the morning which is both a holy and frightening hour
As the heathen then are judged on this day of wrath
And the remnant finds protection under the Shepherd's staff.

Mercy was poured out, compassion beyond compare,

Jesus stands at Calvary waiting for you to meet Him there.

Becoming part of God's remnant is the only preparation for the end;

Our time is short for on the horizon there is blowing a swirling wind.

"For the day of the LORD of hosts shall be upon every one that is proud and lofty, and upon every one that is lifted up; and he shall be brought low:"
(Isaiah 2:12)

"Behold, a whirlwind of the LORD is gone forth in fury, even a grievous whirlwind: it shall fall grievously upon the head of the wicked."
(Jeremiah 23:19)

"On January 20, 2001, President George W. Bush during his first inaugural address faced the obelisk known as the Washington Monument and twice referred to an angel that 'rides in the whirlwind and directs this storm.' His reference was credited to Virginia statesman John Page who wrote to Thomas Jefferson after the Declaration of Independence was signed, saying, 'We know the race is not to the swift nor the battle to the strong. Do you not think an angel rides in the whirlwind and directs this storm?'"

By Thomas R. Horn April 28, 2009 NewsWithViews.com

THE BLACK HOLE

In a place of darkness called the Bohemian Grove
an evil ritual is taking place.
These rituals aren't for entertainment; they purpose the
darkness to trace.
As the darkness rises the minds and eyes of men
are increasingly blind
To the ebbing darkness and the demons
that have been assigned.

Following their assignments
the demons have infiltrated
the minds of men
Imposing confusion, bitterness
and false hatred into them.
People now believing they stand for a righteous cause
but doing the work of evil Jinn.
Those with eyes to see know the darkness is swelling and
a great evil has left its den.

The darkness is marching on our streets; you can hear

the rumble and clatter;
This darkness has many names—one is called
"Black Lives Matter."
Many within this movement want to believe
they stand for a cause,
But they are being played as pawns and are gripped and
wounded by Satan's claws.

Hate is not the answer to the problems
replete among mankind;
The Bible says that Jesus died for all
and none should be maligned.
But those who don't know the living God
do not know of love;
Blind and lost they seek earthly solutions
rather than look above.

More names than I can tell this dark ritual has
summoned from the pit.
Perhaps you've heard of the NWO, Boko Haram, ISIS,
or others that evil foment?
Now you might think me a conspiracy nut
just making foolish noise,
But evil is clearly described as one who kills, who steals
and who destroys.

Evil has been loosed and a growing darkness is
choking the masses,
And in their blindness the people march into
malefic black morasses.
An insatiable morass devours all common sense and
ravages the soul,
And a "Day of Rage" for this nation will become a
ravenous black hole.

A black hole we will enter with little hope of escape
Changing the world we know, its people and landscape.
As the Hegelian Dialectic unfolds without resistance
before our very eyes,
Will the people of God humble themselves
and on their knees to heaven cry?

Or will we chase an imaginary Pokeman
and run after our fantasies
While from the black hole comes persecution
for any who believe
In the Living God of all creation, as excuse is made for
those who build their spires.
The Watchmen weep and the prophets cry
for they know there is a coming fire.

"But the heavens and the earth, which are now, by the same word are kept in store, reserved unto fire against the Day of Judgment and perdition of ungodly men." (2 Peter 3:7)

"Therefore shall her plagues come in one day, death, and mourning, and famine; and she shall be utterly burned with fire: for strong is the Lord God who judgeth her." (Revelation 18:8)

THE DATA

Suddenly everything is all about the data.
We're no longer people; rather we are fodder for the beta—
The beta testing for those who desire to program the masses
And we are just a byte and bit that through the computer passes.

The data has become the gold and silver of tomorrow
And the data will rule our lives and be the cause of sorrow.
It will determine what we are allowed and what we are denied
And from the governed control of your life you will not hide.

Every purchase, every search, everything you post
Is continually collected and your privacy has been revoked.
The data will determine where you are allowed to reside.
The data will determine what you're allowed to sell or buy.

The data will determine the career you are to undertake.
The data will determine when you sleep and when you wake.

The data will determine what type of car you are
allowed to drive.
The data will determine who will live and who will die.

The data has become the gold and silver of today;
It is the measure by which we all are weighed.
Soon the data will determine your husband or your wife;
The data has determined every aspect of every life.

The data has become the most sought asset on the
globe.
The data has become the driving force of secret probes.
The data has become the weapon of mass destruction.
The data is now our Orwellian induction.

There are no more children born, no people left;
We are bytes and bits and our souls have suffered theft.
The collection and flow of data is a primary reason for AI,
And regardless of the rhetoric this is the purpose that
underlies.

Quantum computing with AI control is at our door
And to insure our compliance will be Data Enforcement
Corps,
For he who controls the data will control all men.
The data has become our pathway to our end.

*"We are probably one of the last generations of homo
sapiens. Within a century or two Earth will be dominated
by entities that are more different from us than we are
different from Neanderthals or chimpanzees. Because in
the coming generations we will learn how to engineer
body and brain and mind. This will be the main product
of the economy of the 21st century economy. Not textiles
and vehicles and weapons but body and brain and mind.
Now how exactly will the future masters of the planet
look like? This will be decided by the people who own the
data. Those who control the data control the future not
just of humanity, but the future of life itself. Because
today data is the most important asset in the world."
Yuval Noah Harari from his speech at the World
Economic Forum in Davos, Switzerland in 2018.*

THE DIRECTION OF DESTRUCTION

We are moving steadily in the Direction of Destruction,
The majority ignoring any warning, ignoring all
instruction.
The bodies of children and the souls of men suffer
abduction,
And the world moves forward in the Direction of
Destruction.

Did you see the signs posted along the way?
Mene, Mene, Tekel, Upharsin is what they say.
By the message of truth none seem to be swayed,
And in the direction of destruction we continue to stay.

To stand aside and allow unrestrained murder in the
womb,
To deny these tiny flowers even the opportunity to
bloom
Has tainted the ground and made the earth a worldwide
tomb.
And the Direction of Destruction will lead us to our
doom.

A mother kills her ten-year-old child and states,
"This is not murder, but abortion; I just decided late."
And the 25 civilizations of history that sacrificed their
own
Don't compare to the Direction of Destruction we have
known.

To embrace the lies as though they were truth is our practice,
And too many who are called are voiceless because they are backless.
It is time to grow a spine and forget all political correctness,
For the Direction of Destruction is leading to an eternal blackness.

Men and women of conviction are condemned for
having an opposing opinion,
While the powers that want to be send out their evil
minions
To either kill or harass any opposition to secure their
own dominion,
And the Direction of Destruction makes a nation
become a prison.

The divide between the people is getting wider every
day;
The media owns the minds of men controlling them
by what they say.
A devastating total world war seems to be racing on
its way;
Even Russia says America's Direction of Destruction
was furthered today.

Our direction has done irreparable damage to the
economy
While GMO's have utterly destroyed our agronomy.
Will the great "disclosure" change our perception of
astronomy?
This Direction of Destruction is repeated history;
we're not living an anomaly.

Our robot Overlords have long been designed,
Ready to take over when AI has been refined.
And to the Artilect wars our future has been resigned

While the Direction of Destruction by technology has been aligned.

Every thought of man, as in the days of Noah, is now profane;
There is no action, no deed, no desire that is abstained.
The primary goal of this generation is material wealth and social fame,
And continuing in this Direction of Destruction will prove to be our bane.

Education has become a center for liberalism, socialism and indoctrination
While globally, fools ignore the Islamafication of the nations.
Masculinity is under fierce attack and suffering castration,
And the Direction of Destruction has reached its term of gestation.

We will not be destroyed by the enemy without, or even an EMP;
We will be destroyed by the enemy within—a deadly CMP.
The quest of world leaders is to have **C**ontrol, **M**oney and **P**ower,
And the Direction of Destruction has led us to the final hour.

There is a way that seems right to a man but the end
leads to destruction;
And to the plans of destruction, God has placed His
own Son as an obstruction.
By repentance we can be made like Him and through
Jesus find incorruption;
It requires that we deny the seduction to follow the
Direction of Destruction.

*"There is a way that seemeth right unto a man, but the
end thereof are the ways of death."*
(Proverbs 16:25)

THE FORGOTTEN PLEDGE
TO A FORGOTTEN COUNTRY

I pledge allegiance to the flag

> (Are there men left who will hold true to a pledge?
> We have become a people of lies led by liars.)

Of the United States of America

> (Are we any longer individual states in union or are
> we all subjects of the Federal government?)

And to the Republic

> (Our Republic is gone and a corporation stands in its
> place attempting to placate the masses with de facto
> rule.)

For which it stands

> (The flag can only stand for something if the people
> stand for something; the people no longer stand for
> anything and the Nation has fallen.)

One Nation under God

(Are we a nation? A nation must have borders which we do not, and we are not under God, but we have put God under–under our feet, under our selfish desires, under the dust of the memories of a once great nation.)

Indivisible

(We are grossly divided and the division grows wider each day.)

With liberty

> (Liberty like America past is now a memory; liberty left when we evicted God from our Nation.)

And justice for all

> (Justice vanished with liberty and with God. Justice is only found in the justice of God Almighty and a righteous people who follow that God. "For all" only includes the politically chosen)

The pledge of allegiance to the flag, though not part of our founding documents reiterated the patriotic feelings of most Americans. It is now but a forgotten verse, part of the history of a once great nation that marched into destruction, as did all the great nations of history. We marched into destruction. We did not fall. To fall would imply that it was without intent. Our destruction has come with intent. The one element all great nations of history had in common was their destruction and demise came with the loss of morals, the loss of integrity, the loss of liberties and the loss of faith in God. Alex de Tocqueville said, "America is great because she is good. If America ceases to be good, America will cease to be great." When America finds God, we will once again find the forgotten America.

THE GAMES OF NATIONS:
THE PLAYERS AND THE PLAYED

Politicians are playing games with the lives of the
masses without remorse,
And many of **them** were also played when you track
their successes to its source.
And the games go on day after day.
Can we believe half of what we see or anything they
say?

Scandal and death follow the lives of leaders like a
plague;
The truth behind the fallen in their wake is obscure
and vague.
Those who seek to expose the truth are scandalized
or dead;
So many lies, theories and stories it makes brave
men fear to tread.

There is treason and treachery by those we have
voted for and trusted,
And yet those who stand for righteousness are the
only ones accosted.
How many government branches and agencies
operate outside of their designated purview?

To control the masses, appointed and elected
officials are playing The Taming of the Shrew.

So many questions remain unanswered regarding
office holders and candidates;
Those who would seek the answers are labeled
terrorist and put into the "database."

Eligibility, acts of treason and cover-ups are all a part
of the game that's played.
"Wanting" will be the results when in the balance
the players are ultimately weighed.

But the players are just pieces, movable parts in a
much bigger game
Played by hidden faces, with a dark agenda, from
which they will not refrain.
The game stays the same and has been played for
eons, only the players change;
This Luciferian agenda to devour and destroy always
has remained.

The Republic of the United States, by mystical orders,
was long ago usurped,
And like other empires of history we have become an
historical excerpt.

Empires and nations from age to age have risen and
have fallen,
And the powers elite has always been Satan's
personal golems.

Money changes hands while people are bought and
sold,
And the moneychangers are obsessed with the
desire for more control.
The people suffer daily while the elitists prepare and
hoard their gold,
But there is something changing for the final bell of
this age has tolled.

Political playing is a worldwide phenomenon, but
America has perfected the game.
The Elite and the Electorate, the evil roots and rules
of the contest all remain unchanged.
A contest between good and evil where the innocent
are played,
And now the judging hand of God is coming; it will no
more be stayed.

Whether you are a player or one who is being
played, it makes no difference;
From the coming judgment there is but one sure
source of deliverance.

There is coming a righteous judge to judge the
players and the played,
And deliverance is reserved for those who repented
when they prayed.

Politicians stand before us with their mouths
spewing rehearsed rhetoric.
Are they controlled by unseen forces? Are they
righteous or chimeric?
World leaders playing war games and their own
subjects are the pawns,
And the skies have become darkened being filled
with huge black swans.

The events of tomorrow will be unlike any ever
before,
And were the days not shortened man would be no
more.

I refuse to be played; I will rather fight with armor
and a sword
Than to fall a victim of this orchestrated game—this
unholy dissonant chord.

The game played by the powers of the air will come
to its demise

When the appointed time has come and our Lord breaks through the skies.
Christ will put an end to the evil games and to war and strife,
But woe to those whose names are not found in His Book of Life.

Today and again tomorrow we will be faced with choices we must make,
But soon the time for choices will be done and for many it will be too late...
Too late to repent, too late to accept the free gift that God has offered,
And what does it profit to lose your soul to fill your earthly coffers?

Politics and the game of it is looking for a physical solution in a carnal institution,
But Spiritual problems cannot be solved with natural carnal resolution.
Today, laid before the gamers and the gamed, is the same choice of life or death.
Choose you this day whom you will serve, but as for me and my house,
We will serve the Lord until our final breath.

"And the LORD thy God will make thee plenteous in every work of thine hand, in the fruit of thy body, and in the fruit of thy cattle, and in the fruit of thy land, for good: for the LORD will again rejoice over thee for good, as he rejoiced over thy fathers: If thou shalt hearken unto the voice of the LORD thy God, to keep his commandments and his statutes which are written in this book of the law, and if thou turn unto the LORD thy God with all thine heart, and with all thy soul. For this commandment which I command thee this day, it is not hidden from thee, neither is it far off. It is not in heaven, that thou shouldest say, Who shall go up for us to heaven, and bring it unto us, that we may hear it, and do it? Neither is it beyond the sea, that thou shouldest say, Who shall go over the sea for us, and bring it unto us, that we may hear it, and do it? But the word is very nigh unto thee, in thy mouth, and in thy heart, that thou mayest do it. See, I have set before thee this day life and good, and death and evil; In that I command thee this day to love the LORD thy God, to walk in his ways, and to keep his commandments and his statutes and his judgments, that thou mayest live and multiply: and the LORD thy God shall bless thee in the land whither thou goest to possess it. But if thine heart turn away, so that thou wilt not hear, but shalt be drawn away, and worship other gods, and serve them; I denounce unto you this day, that ye shall surely perish, and that ye shall not prolong your

days upon the land, whither thou passest over Jordan to go to possess it. I call heaven and earth to record this day against you, that I have set before you life and death, blessing and cursing: therefore choose life, that both thou and thy seed may live."
 (Deuteronomy 30:9-19)

THE HEADLINES

I took a look at the headlines today;
I was interested in what they had to say.
Before I could get through them I had to stop and pray;
It appears by the news we haven't many more days.

It seems treason is rampant across the nation
From the very lowest to the highest stations.
Censorship has become completely out of control,
And only the Christian or conservative voice is put on hold.

Strange creatures popping up in home security cameras,
And soy boys wearing lace thinking they are glamorous.
I couldn't find a positive report regarding finances–
Just a million lies to ensure a few get personal advances.

It was reported that people were dying in clusters–
Such strange events; we might need the Ghostbusters.
Speaking of paranormal it seems were close to disclosure,
But when aliens are presented we will suffer from such exposure.

The tar pits are boiling and volcanoes are no longer dormant;
The media desires to crucify any truthful informant.

This has happened before in man's history—
Truth was crucified at Calvary.

Ebola or maybe "Disease X" is on the rise;
The attack continues unabated on our skies.
You ask why I said maybe, it is because of what I've learned;
Lies are not uncommon when a pandemic is concerned.
The LGBTQ army is fighting for control,
And to legalize pedophilia is their goal.
Sanctuary states and cities defy the law,
And from every headline I see the marks of Satan's claws.

Once again the west is set on fire;
Elsewhere the floodwaters are rising higher.
The weather wars have been unleashed,
And now I'm afraid to continue to read.

One headline reported of a strange "one-eye" sign—
An occult symbol extremely prevalent in our times,
Important to those believing they are chosen bloodlines
While in Jerusalem the intent is to build a Temple Shrine.

One report I thought would be entertaining,
But to my spirit it was draining.
It was a report about an old show on TV,

And it seems it was more than fiction; we are sustenance
for the "V."

It seems that maybe the moon is shrinking;
In the south a city is sinking.
The children are no longer taught critical thinking,
And an odor from "Hellywood" is stinking.

The political divide is exponentially growing;
The elite are becoming worried, knowing
That a little more exposure is all it will take
Until the **masses**, not just the few, become awake.

In the church house a New Age demon resides;
On staff are mediums introducing Spirit Guides.
Other gods isn't something the True and Living God will
abide,
And Clergy Response Teams will be cause for a great
divide.

People have become lovers of themselves, lovers of
money, boastful, proud, abusive, disobedient to their
parents, ungrateful, unholy,
Without love, unforgiving, slanderous, without self-
control, brutal, not lovers of the good; this is our world
now not something happening slowly.

Can judgment wait much longer when you consider the
headlines and the state we're in?
Judgment begins in God's own house and it is coming
unless God's people repent of sin.

I took a look at the headlines today;
I was interested in what they had to say.
Before I could get through them I had to stop and pray;
It appears by the news we haven't many more days.

If you think these reports all foolishness and conspiracy,
Then your mind is clouded just the way principalities
want it to be.
People will perish for a lack of knowledge,
And a delusion places the mind in bondage.

The world is changing but God does not change.
He is the only hope no matter how strange
The world becomes—not just the headlines.
Shake off your bias and see the signs.

He is an ever-present help in times of trouble;
Soon this world will become nothing more than rubble.
Repentance is the master key to your survival
Because the headlines won't change unless there is
revival.

"God is our refuge and strength, a well-proven help in trouble. Therefore we will not fear, though the earth be removed, and though the mountains be carried into the midst of the sea; though its waters roar and foam, though the mountains shake with its swelling."
(Psalm 46:1-3)
"... call on Me in the day of trouble; I will deliver you and you will glorify Me."
(Psalm 50:15)

THE LOST GENERATION

The Lost Generation has been subjected to Hell's
penetration,
And when they were forbidden to pray they lost their
way.
I think more than lost their way; they were purposely led
astray—
A maleficent inception so that they are given over to
deception,

Revisionist history so the past is then a mystery.
To control the future, alas, you only need to hide the
past.
This dark and evil intrusion brought to them gender
confusion—
Not knowing who they are, living vicariously through
avatars.

Those who did not fall to deception's call
Will be the victims of extermination via vaccination.
By their own perversion they are perplexed until they all
are vexed,
Living in denial, unable to face life's simplest trials.

The Lost Generation is subjected to Hell's penetration;
"I-Phonery" dependent to whom technology is
transcendent.
Subjected to pedophilia from the pit which has
consumed the body politic,

Living with satanic scars, what will be revealed in their memoirs?

Common Core was introduced so that a generation would be seduced,
Believing socialism is to be sought and gender confusion should be taught.
Undermining the family and their freedom is an agenda to mislead them;
A generation now ignorant of the truth, fulfilling the illuminists' goal to own the youth.

MK Ultra mind control is the stealing of someone's soul.
How many in our classrooms have been for deception groomed?
The truth is not readily accepted, for normalcy bias the truth has intercepted;
Then the media reports to ensure that we used "conspiracy theory" to obscure.

Environmentalists adhere to religious tenets, even to the earth paying penance.
Scripted actors spout the environmental liturgy, ignoring definitive science or history.
The Lost Generation absorbs their every word, unaware the truth has been blurred.
Soon the Lost Generation will become world rulers and Agenda 2030 has become our future.

There will be judgment and those to blame will pay for the generation that was led astray,

Always providing a new game to play rather than teaching them how to pray.
Now we give them to AI demon-possessed machines, their faces constantly glued to screens
Introducing them to things that have become their nightmare scenes.

The stuff that nightmares are made of is their inheritance rather than love.
Will the "cannibots" now be sent; will the powers that be ever repent?
What evil have we given for this generation to embrace; what is the future of the human race?
In a world without God it is no wonder they eat soap pods...

Unequipped to face life's problems they resort to snorting condoms.
Snowflakes melting in the heat while they're marching in the streets,
Unaware that it is our bane that the unborn without mercy are being slain.
A generation has lost its way because we declared they could no longer pray.

Who gave them Values Clarification and did so without hesitation?
Who told them there were no absolutes rather than providing them the truth?
Were we really so unaware when we employed college professors like Bill Ayers—

Rules for Radicals being taught, proclaiming it to be progressive thought?

Who gave out condoms completely unbridled and who took away the Bible?
As parents we must accept some blame; we were too busy to understand their game.
We believed the educators and gave enormous trust and they betrayed it for their own lusts.
It would be better if a stone were around their necks than to have caused this generational wreck.

What are your children being taught? The answer to this question must be sought.
Meditation and Eastern Mysticism is "OK," but from the Truth you must stay away.
Visit a mosque to broaden your horizons, but stay away from Jesus or they sound the PC siren!
Blame becomes irrelevant, rescue is now the goal; pray that the broken pieces can become whole.

They're forced to breathe poison air; I wonder is there anyone who cares.
Toxic water they have to drink and they haven't the skills to critically think.
Their food has no nutrition by design and the RF waves pound their minds.
Broken homes are the rule, children left to face a world that's cruel.

This begs a question that must be asked, "Who is responsible for the evil that has amassed?"
Was the Church also busy at play when we should have been leading the way?
Is it fair to say too many in the churches failed to pray While a world was led astray spiraling downward in decay?

THE SEASON OF BLOOD

We are a people obsessed with blood;
Entertainment brings it to us with a flood.
Many believe their dark TV series are all about love,
But vampires my friends are all about blood.

Blood was shed in order to cover the nakedness of man;
For offerings priests would shed the blood of a lamb.
Abel's blood still cries out from the ground;
Today the blood soaked soil makes a deafening sound.

Bloodletting was once thought to bring healing,
But the life is in the blood and that has multiple meanings.
We sing, "There is power in the blood," but do we believe our song?
The Illuminist believes the blood will make him strong.

There are cultures that drink the blood of their enemy;
They consume the blood as part of an ancient alchemy.
But it is not as ancient as you might think;
Just today there were those that blood did drink.

We are a people of blood with blood on our hands;
Blood stains our clothes and blood stains our land.
Blood is shed for the cheapest and the vilest of reasons;

From the seats of power blood is shed with malfeasance.

Jesus shed His blood as an ultimate and final sacrifice;
No other blood is needed and no other blood will
suffice…
Suffice to wash away the sins of all mankind,
But darkness has intruded and deluded men's minds.

Men believe they can control the power of the blood
themselves,
And so dark rituals and death are brought up from the
pit of hell.
The war over blood started in the Garden of God with
Eve;
That is what is meant by enmity that was to be between
the seed.

To corrupt the blood has been the goal of all ages
Because corrupted blood could not possibly save us.
Corruption of the blood can be realized in altering the
DNA,
And corruption of the seed as in the days of Noah goes
on today.

Adrenochrome should not even be a word within our
language;

In order to obtain it children are adrenalized and
tortured into anguish.
Then those dark practitioners ingest it with anticipation
 Of eternal youth, but they will find it brings eternal
damnation.

The abortion industry has changed us into a people of
blood;
It is the antithesis of Truth and we are guilty of innocent
blood.
For the flesh there are many functions performed by the
blood,
But for the Spirit there is no virtue in the shedding of
innocent blood.

Will our obsession with blood be satisfied
When blood runs in the streets four feet high,
When the dead outnumber all the mothers' tears,
And just to bury them will take over seven years?

And those who are not washed clean by His blood
May find in that day that they will be drowned in blood.
The blood of Jesus, when it was spilled, tore the veil in
the temple in two,
And today there are those who attempt to mend the veil
like new,

Striving to rebuild a temple to sacrifice animals again
upon the altar.
But God says, "Bring no more vain offerings;" He will not
listen to the psalter.
God asks, "For what purpose is the multitude of your
sacrifices to Me?"
"It is finished" is the cry that was heard when Jesus'
bloodstained the tree.

Every thought of man is now consumed with plans for
evil—
Within every home, every government and under every
steeple.
To make personal gain at the cost of blood is now
routine,
And coming soon to your dinner table will be Soylent
Green.

Corrupted blood, shed blood, innocent blood,
Bloodstains, bloodguilt, blood mixed in the mud;
Rivers of blood, oceans of blood, blood to the horse's
bridle,
For we are suicidal and homicidal in a world that is
genocidal.

It has always been all about the blood and it still is today;
There are those under the altar waiting for their blood to be repaid.
The judgment Hand of the Most High God will not always be stayed,
And those unrepentant with blood still on their hands should be very afraid.

We are now in "The Season Of Blood"; the times have become dark.
Soon the blood will be shed of those who refuse to take the mark.
Those who are possessed by corrupted blood are obsessed with shedding it,
And the enmity that was spoken of between the seed line still exists.

Your corrupted DNA can be changed, but you must be re-born.
With repentance comes a cleansing flow; it is from Calvary borne.
The shed blood of Jesus Christ was and is the sufficient sacrifice;
Any other letting of blood is a dark counterfeit used to entice...

To entice men to seek a forbidden knowledge and
power,
And men engage the darkness unaware of the hour.
Whether unaware or in defiance men drink the blood,
But blood will not forever be unavenged and many will
die in the guilt of their own blood.

*"When you reach out your hands, I will hide My eyes
from you; even when you make many prayers,
I will not hear. Your hands are full of blood."
(Isaiah 1:15, Isaiah 1:11-20, Revelation 9:10-11, John
19:30)*

THE SYMPTOMS OF AMERICA'S DISEASE

The secret to the future of America's survival
Is not found in Washington, but in the pages of the Bible.
There is no hope in the acts of men who hold high
position;
Hope is in the hearts of men when there is true
contrition.

Abortion is not America's problem, but only a revealing
symptom—
A symptom of a larger problem that is growing with
intention:
Intentions to destroy countless generations of unknown
greatness,
Symptoms of an affliction grown from Satan's heart fed
with hellish execration.

To stop abortion is indeed a necessary, godly and noble
calling,
But it is not the solution to America's rapid spiral falling.
In part, our downward spiral is because innocent babes
were sacrificed.
The babies die, and our nation, because we trade the
truth for lies.

Putting a stop to the production of all insidious pornography,
Though needed, will not alone change our nation's destiny.
For like abortion, the issue of porn is a symptom of an illness
Which left untreated will grow worse until it eventually kills us.

We must boldly speak the truth exposing this destroyer
Consuming families and generations addicted to being voyeurs.
But the cure is not found in medicating another symptom;
To treat the disease the symptom reveals must be our intention.

The economy is failing, the stock market is unsure,
The jobless rate is increasing. Can America endure?
To end the debt, control our spending, and live on easy street
Will not save America because debt is not the reason for our defeat.

Slavery is rampant; there are murders by the score.
Evil men are greedy and continually wanting more.
Gangs rule the streets where once it was safe to roam,

And families live in boxes because they have lost their homes.

Darkness and drugs, with addicts adding burden to society,
Children left abandoned and abused; there are no parental priorities.
We declared a "war on drugs," but we don't use the proper weapons for the fight.
We have abandoned spiritual weapons and given the battle to the night.

There are so many more symptoms that could be exemplified
And we scarce can count the numbers of the men who've died
From the disease of sin that has now infected all of man.
We accept the symptoms, ignore the disease and follow Satan's plan.

The only hope for America's future survival
Is not found in removing symptoms, but in praying for revival.
The parchment of the scroll of God must now be unfurled;
The message that heals the nation is to the church and not the world.

To sin we are resigned and God warned of the results
that sin has left behind:
A nation living now in darkness where it seems all men
are blind,
The symptoms of a world where Satan has had his way,
The symptoms of a world where the church has been at
play.

The healing of a nation is left to the body of Christ;
With repentance from the people of God there will be
new life.
The world is not called to humility or to turn away;
The call is to the bride of Christ to be humble and pray.

When the bride is spotless, God will perform a mighty
feat;
The symptoms of sin's disease will flee with a healing
that's complete.
The promises of God will never fail and He will heal our
land,
But the time is growing short for His coming is at hand.

*"And, behold, I come quickly; and my reward is with me,
to give every man according as his work shall be."
(Revelation 22:12)*

TOO MUCH TOO LITTLE

Americans are **too insulated** to believe we can be
inconvenienced by a war upon our shores.

We are **too addicted** to our sins to ever lament
or give them to Jesus and repent.

Too much of the church is **too Biblically illiterate** to
recognize the truth or to discern the lies.

Americans are **too ingrained** in their cognitive
dissonance to engage and make a difference.

Too many people are **too afraid** to leave their normalcy
bias to believe there are coming bloody riots.

Most are **too blind** to see and **too deaf** to hear the call
of the watchmen who have been standing on the wall.

And countless will find the hour is much **too late**
when they finally become awake,

For already death has climbed through our windows and
cut off the children from the streets,
and the unbelievers now **too late** begin to weep.

And the words of the prophet Jeremiah will haunt their
nights and torment their days,
*"The harvest is past, the summer has ended, and we
are not saved."*
(Jeremiah. 8:20)

CONCLUSION

Though the days appear to be days of trouble (and at times more than just appear), for many of us the economic situation is at our door. Many are facing physical hardships or emotional crises. The moral state of our nation is in ruin, the education system in decline, marriage is under attack, natural disasters loom at the door, the global warming prophets of doom cry louder each day, there are wars, famine and poverty around the globe, and on and on we could go speaking of the decline of our nation and our world. But what is our response to today's world?

God told Joshua to "fear not" but that's often easier said than done. Is there another response? The answer is YES! God's promise to us is that He will never leave us or forsake us.

When we became a nation 240-plus years ago, God was there; when Columbus left Spain to discover a new world 526 years ago (He wasn't the first), God was there; and when Rome ruled the world supremely over 2,000 years ago, God was there.

Add another three hundred years or so when Alexander conquered the known world, God was there. Go back 2,600 years when the Medes and Persians ruled, and God was there. Continue this journey almost 3,600 years ago when Moses was born in Egypt, and God was there. Around 4,000 years ago when Abraham left his home for a land he did not know, God was there.

Back to the garden where Adam appeared upon this earth—God was there! Throughout all the history of man God has been there. Through all the wars and hatred and turbulence of history God has been there.

Today is no different than the past. Trouble has been with man since the fall; it came with the curse. We all too often blame Adam for our misery, but are not all men Adam? Are we not created in the image of God and yet we are full of rebellion and disobey God? The good news is God loves us anyway, just as He loved Adam, and He is still here, and will be here until, as the Bible puts it, "even to the end of time."

So, what does that mean?

It means God is still setting captives free, His grace is still sufficient, His mercy is still without limit, He is still making the lame to walk and the blind to see, and His free gift of love is still available to all who will seek Him.

Regardless of what the world looks like on the evening news, and regardless of what the world looks like in the confines of your own house, God is still on the throne! His word says, "I have never seen the righteous forsaken or their children begging for bread."

God's promise isn't to remove the storms of life but to walk with us through them. But if you reject the free gift of God, you reject His Strong Arm and provision for the storms that lay not in the distant future, but at our door.

Without Him you will not survive the days ahead and you will suffer your rejection for eternity.

Today is the day of salvation. As we have looked at the provision of salvation through the cross, the journey of life which is the journey to the cross, and the eyewitnesses of the crucifixion who saw the cross as no one else in all of history, I pray you are considering what choice you will make concerning the sacrifice of Calvary and the person of Jesus Christ. If you are questioning, please look to the back of the book where you will find a prayer for accepting Jesus as your Savior.

CHAPTER TWO
ABORTION

HE WILL WIPE EVERY TEAR FROM THEIR EYES

Last night as I lay sleeping I had a troubling dream
In the morning when I awoke I relived every scene.
I dreamt that I was in heaven and saw children as far as
the eye could see—
Babes in every direction completely surrounding me.

They were everyone weeping, crying sorrowful
streaming tears.
Suddenly in the midst of this crowd a heavenly being
appeared.
He called out to the children as at his presence they all
drew near.
He said, "Be patient little ones for He is almost here."

I approached this magnificent creature to ask permission
to inquire,
"What has happened here; what tragedy has
transpired?"
Stretching out his arms in a giant sweeping motion

He replied, "These are children never born, the victims of abortion."

Again I risked to question and asked, "Why do they cry?"
He dropped his head and then answered with a sigh, "They weep for a lifetime of losses that are poured out on them in a single moment.
The missed joys and pains, struggles and victories coming all at once are raw and potent."

"But is this not heaven?" I asked, and I thought in heaven you weren't supposed to cry.
"You are close child, but there are tears; the difference is Jesus will wipe every tear from every eye."
Looking at this ocean of children I was overcome by the sheer magnitude of its size.
And deep within my spirit anger, sadness and confusion began to rise.

The angel pointed to a redheaded, freckled boy that looked a little roughish.
He said, "This one was to have two sons that he would teach to hunt and fish."
And indicating towards a little girl, he spoke of a discovery she was supposed to make.
All were crying for a purpose on earth that will never be fulfilled and for breath they'll never take.

I noticed some were sobbing violently; they seemed more hurt than some of the others.
The angel pulled one close and said, "These are late-term abortions and for 9 months they knew their mother.
But they never felt her arms around them and were never held to her breast;
They knew her voice and anticipated—then suddenly from her they were wrest!"

I realized these millions of lives were more than single tragedies,
It is exponential when you start adding up the casualties.
The world has experienced casualties and losses of which it will never know—
Life touching life, touching life, touching life that now can never grow.

I fell to my knees before the children praying that Jesus would get there soon,
But in that same instant I suddenly awoke and found myself back in my room.
I know that He is comforting those whom for Molech were taken before their time,
And I fear for the coming judgment because we have tolerated this shameful heinous crime.

"For the Lamb which is in the midst of the throne shall feed them, and shall lead them unto living fountains of waters: and God shall wipe away all tears from their eyes."
(Revelation 7:17)

I STILL CRY WHEN I'M ALONE

I still cry when I'm alone;
No one told me it would be like this.
I long to hold my child and give a mother's kiss;
No one told me it was a child I'd miss.

I still cry alone at night;
They said it was just tissue, not a life.
This pain, will it ever go away?
My tears run free, they cannot be stayed.

I still cry when I'm alone—
My empty house, my empty home.
A child cries from an unknown grave;
My child aborted, an innocent babe.

I still cry alone at night;

The truth I traded for a lie.

The lie was born where evil roams;

I clutched the lie till it was my own.

I still cry when I'm alone;

A life is gone and my heart groans

From empty arms and my own desire.

My soul still burns; it is on fire.

I still cry when I'm alone—

No chance to live, no chance to grow.

I have hope, for Jesus has forgiven all my past,

But how long will this feeling last?

I still cry when I'm alone.

"And you, that were sometime alienated and enemies in your mind by wicked works, yet now hath he reconciled In the body of his flesh through death, to present you holy and unblameable and unreproveable in his sight:" (Colossians 1:21-22)

I WAS A CHILD

To swing from a rope hanging in a tree,
To play in a puddle pretending it's the sea,
To be the sheriff of an old western town,
Or paint my face like I was a clown,

I'll never do these simple things;
They are confined to dwell in my dreams.
I wasn't allowed laughter, play, or even breath;
Before I was born I met with death.

To hear a fine story while in mother's lap,
To have milk and cookies just before nap,
To open a present and play party games,
To have a pat on my head and be called by name,

I'll never know these simple joys.
I'll never play with the neighborhood boys;
No pet dog I could name King or name Spot;
No tears and no laughter because I am not.

I'll never be seen running a race,

I'll never get to run to first base,

I'll never know the thrill of first dates,

No one will worry because I'm out late.

I'll never have a college degree,

I'll never know the shade of a tree,

I'll never throw a lure in the water,

I'll never have my own son or daughter.

I'll never fail and I'll never succeed,

I'll never hurt cause I skinned my knee,

I'll never know the excitement of reading a book,

I'll never hear a babbling brook.

To experience these things you must be alive—

Alas I am not, because of a lie.

I am just tissue so it said in Mom's file,

But I'm more than just tissue; I WAS A CHILD.

"That thou hast slain my children, and delivered them to cause them to pass through the fire for them?"
 (Ezekiel 16:21)

PURPOSES UNFULFILLED

"I know the plans I have for you," words spoken by the
Lord.
Even before we were born, by God we were adored.
All the days of our lives by God himself have been
ordained,
But those plans, lives yet to be lived, and the Word of
God we have disdained.

The plans and purposes of God for many will never be
fulfilled
Because we allowed abortion the plans of God to steal.
A man will never have a wife, for his wife while in the
womb was killed,
And his future children will not be born and their
purpose will not be fulfilled.

A young girl will never have a sister or a brother she will
never know;
She will face childhood without a sibling and it will
change the way she grows.
How many generations will be changed because of the
blood that has been spilled?
And untold lives continue to be denied with purposes
unfulfilled.

It is without question that countless accomplishments have been denied,
The world robbed of unknown miracles because before they were born, they died.
God himself comforts those who were the victims of abortion,
But still they cry for their loss of life, our incredible moral distortion.

In a book that belongs only to the Lord, all our members were written,
But from man's books of law, the Word of God was stricken.
And the love that God has for those who are yet unborn,
By abortion has been blatantly and shamefully scorned.

The earth groans under the weight of the tiny bodies that it holds;
The cries of the unborn shake the heavens to its inner folds.
It is wretched and abominable that tiny body parts are chilled
To preserve them for the market place so that greedy pockets can be filled.

The blood of the aborted cries out and exposes to heaven our appalling guilt,

And the world ignores the cries while shouting wantonly,
"Do as thou wilt!"
Shouting to drown out the cries of the innocent we have killed;
The aborted crying in the arms of Jesus knowing their purpose is unfulfilled.

"For I know the thoughts that I think toward you, saith the LORD, thoughts of peace, and not of evil, to give you an expected end."
(Jeremiah 29:11)

"For thou hast possessed my reins: thou hast covered me in my mother's womb. I will praise thee; for I am fearfully and wonderfully made: marvellous are thy works; and that my soul knoweth right well. My substance was not hid from thee, when I was made in secret, and curiously wrought in the lowest parts of the earth.
Thine eyes did see my substance, yet being unperfect; and in thy book all my members were written, which in continuance were fashioned, when as yet there was none of them. How precious also are thy thoughts unto me, O God! How great is the sum of them!"
(Psalm 139:13-17)

THE TRUTH ABOUT TOLERENCE

The children of today will believe and spread the lies.
The youth of today have been trained in Satan's franchise.
The mothers of today are participants in our destruction.
The fathers of today will be the death of all succumbing to the great seduction.

It started with a simple word—that word is tolerant—
Just ignoring those things that were formerly abhorrent.
Not necessarily agreeing, and perhaps even taking a stand,
But the fathers grew weary and didn't hold the line in the sand.

What one generation will tolerate, the next is sure to embrace.
This condition is prolific amongst the human race,
And now more than embrace, the lies are held as dear.
What comes next is the reality of all your fears.

Forgotten are the words of Jesus, "he that endureth to the end shall be saved."
And "brethren, be not weary in well doing." But too many now have caved.
As the tolerating and embracing continue and grow each passing day,
Destruction comes when each man desires his own way.

There was a time in 1933 when on Jekyll island there was
a travesty,
And the result of that meeting has become too long our
reality.
The Act of 1871 lost our Republic as the founding fathers
warned,
And there was no one to take a stand and none to
mourn.

Political toleration has gone unabated,
And the norm is now those things that formerly were
hated.
Normalcy bias is used to great perfection by the enemy
of our souls,
And great lengths were gone to in order to disguise the
words of ancient scrolls.

Teaching from the church has become a shred of the real
truth,
And we now embrace what once was thought uncouth.
Schools are no longer just places of indoctrination,
But are now literal training grounds for future
confrontation.

In attempting to show headship some fathers rule with
an iron fist;
There is no love or grace, only what they insist.
Where is longsuffering and what becomes of grace?
You cannot be the father you were designed to be unless
you seek His face.

Can you love your son or daughter who has become gay?
You mustn't accept their actions, but must show them
love will stay.
It is a fine line to walk I know, but fine lines are not a
stranger to the believer;
Narrow is the way and few there are who find it, while
others follow a deceiver.

God gave us 10 Commandments and we can't even
follow them,
And men make rules upon rules rather than overcoming
sin.
We give up much too easily or never take a stand at all,
And the resulting effect is clearly apparent as families
and fathers fall.

We must speak out against murder of babies in the
womb;
If we give up the fight we best prepare our tombs.
But there were some who tolerated abortion and the
generations that followed embraced it completely.
And regardless how twisted the rhetoric is, it is set in
their minds concretely.

So now because of those that tolerated, we sacrifice to
the gods of old.
Babies are killed to honor them and the children are
being sold,
Empowering the principalities and powers in another
dimensional place,

Powers that long to be as God and who desire the annihilation of the human race.

If you don't know the truth, then it is hard to fight with conviction,
And we tolerate the apostate as if it were our own addiction.
People perish for lack of knowledge; we don't study to rightly divide truth.
And what the fathers tolerated has been embraced by too many youth.

For example the LGBTQ agenda is more than a sexual preference;
It is the practice of the offspring of the Watchers and we accept it with deference.
You see women were only used for the purpose of procreation,
But for the sons of the Watchers, sodomy was the much-preferred inclination.

As it was in the days of Noah the practices of the Watchers again prevail,
And once again the whole of earth by the Watchers has been derailed.
The knowledge of the Watchers throughout history has been sought,
And those who desire this knowledge will have it at any cost.

To reverse the action of the Watchers when they descended upon the earth
Is why Jesus came and sacrificed Himself and gave to us new birth.
And to seek the Watchers out again is a mockery of His sacrifice;
Tolerating or remaining silent in the presence of evil will not suffice.

It is why the watchmen cry and seek to warn both day and night;
These events have happened before causing suffering and blight.
The things that will come again are more than man has yet imagined;
Men's minds will fall under great delusion until all mankind is maddened.

We must know what we tolerate or we will find that death will be the result,
For the powers and principalities are sought by more than some strange cult.
Disclosure is what I now refer to in this current verse,
And to communicate with extra-terrestrials is constantly rehearsed.

Political correctness has been ingrained into generations now,
And to turn against it will seem to them something they must disavow.

That which they believe as truth is embedded in their
mental core;
This will mean blood, even on the altar, in any coming
war.
Tolerating sin, tolerating lies, tolerating the teachings of
the fallen is the how;
The sins of the fathers are visited upon the generations
that to the lie will bow.
It all goes back to Genesis—every evil plan and every lying
god—
It has happened over and over that by the fallen ones
man is awed.

Whether through some magic incantation or Babalon
Working,
Behind the terrors that men face today, Satan and his
fallen ones are lurking.
Every evil intent from geo-engineering to poisoning our
food and water
Is part of a master plan, the human race to slaughter.

It is imperative that we teach our sons and we teach our
daughters
Who is the father of lies and about our Heavenly Father.
God is our only hope in these times of trouble;
Tolerance will only result in a world reduced to rubble.

Jesus is the answer; there is no other name by which
men can be saved.
It is by rejecting Jesus that mankind becomes depraved.
As it was in the days of Noah, so shall it be again,

And you've already been deluded if you're waiting for that to begin.

"There is no salvation in any other, for there is no other name under heaven given among men by which we must be saved."
(Acts 4:12)

THE WAR UPON THE WOMB

In the valley of Hinnom at Tophet, overlooking
Jerusalem, stood the image of Molech.
With a fire in his belly, the people bring their children
to his brazen arms outstretched.
This is a gruesome story of torture of blood and of
pain;
A story of the time when Baal—or call him Nimrod or
Molech— reigned.

The Devil demands the blood of the innocent and as
the numbers swell,
You can hear from other dimensions the haunting
laughter of hell.
Molech's demands haven't changed from the
beginning until now,
And his followers lay their offerings at his feet and
there they bow.

Mao Zedong continued Molech's reign and fifty-plus
million died.
The world looks back at his butchery, murder and
genocide,
And fools think him a hero for his atrocious crimes;
Others think it doesn't matter, for as at Tophet, it
was another time.

But time does not bind evil and evil continues to demand
The blood of the children and the seed of the man.
We could add Pol Pot, Stalin and Lenin to this list;
Hitler and Minh and Mussolini should not be missed.

Ante Pavelic, Charles Taylor, Foday Sankoh and Idi Amin—
All butchers and tyrants so it would seem.
They continued the practice of heinous torture and
shedding the blood of the innocent,
Killing the men and the women, the children and even
the infants.

If we knew of their plans, would we allow their crimes to
take place?
Would we speak of righteousness and put evil in its
place?
Would Mullah Omar, Hideki, Tito or Hussein
Be allowed to commit acts brutal and profane?

Jean Kambanda, Leonid Breznev, Gowon, or Kim IL
Sung—
For their victims in the ground, does justice have a
tongue?
Men consumed with ruling every people and every
nation;
Men who have fallen to Nimrod's ancient temptation.

Did I mention that Nimrod sacrificed seventy thousand children to the fire?
To build Babylon, the Mother of Harlots, was his desire.
The religion taught by the fallen ones through time continues to survive;
The abominations of the earth still breathe and have never died.

Pinochet, Leopold and the Young Turks of the Ottoman Empire
All played their part in feeding Molech's belly fire.
Today we reel in disbelief of ISIS and their grotesque actions,
But the ocean of blood from all these combined has not brought the Fallen satisfaction.

The religion of Babylon grows best in advanced, but Godless civilizations,
And America has given Babylon the perfect habitation.
The Alien world of Winkie Pratney is no longer a fictitious unreality;
It thrives in every city and every street leads to its lethality.

We have become the image of the gods we attend,
And the people deny history and try to pretend

That all of man's evil is natural and just,
So that we can continue to wallow in our lusts.

Babylon is here, Babylon is now and is no longer hidden;
Saturn has taught the mothers to devour their children.
Embryos in plastic sold as paperweights,
The sanctity of life even the mothers unnaturally
desecrate.

Rather than nurtured, the children for profit are
devoured;
Rather than cherished, they are seduced by the hour.
Indifference has taken the place of love and evil rules
men's hearts,
And the fate of the unborn is to be harvested for body
parts.

The slaughter of the innocents is a War upon the Womb,
And America's participation will seal America's tomb.
We hold in esteem such as Margret Sanger and act as if
she is a prima donna,
But with this false esteem we but imitate Gehenna.

The cherished institution of Planned Parenthood has
fomented the loss of maternal instinct,
And if allowed to fulfill Satan's plan, all of humanity will
become extinct.

Is there not a new list of names that could be added to those who possess the spirit of Beelzebub?
It is those in the abortion industry who have stained the entire world with blood.

The War on the Womb has shed more blood and claimed more lives,
Has debauched the nations and told more lies
Than all the evil tyrants listed above and all of world history combined.
Now judgment will surely come and the guilty it will find.

This war is not new or resigned to myth, nor is it confined to theology or eschatology;
It is a spiritual war come to the dimension of man and the forces of darkness are reality.
The slaughter of the innocents is a War upon the Womb,
And America's participation will seal America's tomb.

"Yea, they sacrificed their sons and their daughters unto devils, And shed innocent blood, even the blood of their sons and of their daughters, whom they sacrificed unto the idols of Canaan: and the land was polluted with blood. Thus were they defiled with their own works, and went a whoring with their own inventions.

Therefore was the wrath of the LORD kindled against his people, insomuch that he abhorred his own inheritance. And he gave them into the hand of the heathen; and they that hated them ruled over them."

(Psalm 106:36-41)

THE MESSAGE

The message within the poems about abortion should be regarded more as a message to the nation rather than to individuals who have been lied to, fooled, and who have had an abortion. However, if you as an individual regard the practice of abortion as acceptable then keep reading to see what the Scripture reveals about the shedding of innocent blood; innocent blood is not shed without consequence.

If God heard the blood of Abel crying from the ground after he was murdered by Cain, then the blood of the innocent children, and not just those aborted, but the innocent who are murdered in this nation alone must be a deafening roar in His ears.

I pray that those who have succumbed to the lie do not live in guilt or fear. God is ready, God is willing, and most of all God is able to forgive. You must lean upon Him to find the strength to forgive yourself. There is no condemnation for those who have been forgiven through the blood of Jesus.

"Behold, the LORD'S hand is not shortened, that it cannot save; neither his ear heavy, that it cannot hear: But your iniquities have separated between you and your God, and your sins have hid his face from you, that he will not hear. For your hands are defiled with blood, and your fingers with iniquity; your lips have spoken lies, your tongue hath muttered perverseness. None calleth for justice, nor any pleadeth for truth: they trust in vanity, and speak lies; they conceive mischief, and bring forth iniquity. They hatch cockatrice' eggs, and weave the spider's web: he that eateth of their eggs dieth, and that which is crushed breaketh out into a viper. Their webs shall not become garments, neither shall they cover themselves with their works: their works are works of iniquity, and the act of violence is in their hands. Their feet run to evil, and they make haste to shed innocent blood: their thoughts are thoughts of iniquity; wasting and destruction are in their paths. The way of peace they know not; and there is no judgment in their goings: they have made them crooked paths: whosoever goeth therein shall not know peace. Therefore is judgment far from us, neither doth justice overtake us: we wait for light, but behold obscurity; for brightness, but we walk in darkness."
(Isaiah 59:1-9)

CHAPTER THREE
When I Saw The Cross

WHEN I SAW THE CROSS

When I saw the cross I was ashamed;

Every one there all felt the same.

I fell to the ground, my face in my hands,

Too weak to move, too frail to stand.

I couldn't help but look back to His face,

Wondering how I had come to this place.

I knew what I'd done and I knew where I'd been;

I didn't want to admit this was the price of my sin.

I enjoyed living, being rowdy and free;

I did what I wanted because life was for me,

Or so I thought until life suddenly stopped;

That usually happens when one has been caught...

Caught by the consequences of actions taken,

Caught when integrity has been forsaken,

Caught by my guilt and violently shaken,

Caught by the knowledge in my soul that awakened.

When I saw the cross I was humbled and silent.

I hoped that He knew it was not my intent

To drive nails in His hands or a spear in His side,

But I couldn't convey it; I just lay there and cried.

If you'd seen what I saw when I saw the cross,

You'd understand why I felt totally lost.

Although I saw Jesus, that's not all I could see—

Mostly I saw the person in me.

I wasn't at all as I'd always imagined myself—

Handsome, and famous, and gaining in wealth.

No, I was ugly, alone and exceedingly poor.

I turned away; I could bear it no more,

To see myself the way that I really am;

A wretched example of what is a man.

Jesus spoke, "I've been waiting for you."

Hearing His words I suddenly knew…

The blood, the suffering, and that rugged old tree,

Had all taken place especially for me.

Now I've been redeemed; there's a new man inside.

The old man is gone; in fact he has died.

My life's not the same since I saw the cross;

I count it all gain, not a hint of a loss.

But it wasn't the cross that changed my life;

It was love's greatest gift—God's Son, Jesus Christ.

Dying for sin on an old wooden tree,

I remember he said He was waiting for me.

Conclusion

Salvation was made possible **on** the cross, not **by** the cross. Salvation is made possible only through the person of Jesus Christ, the only begotten Son of the Living God. If you do not have a relationship with Jesus, you can have one today, even right now. If there is any word within the pages of this book that spoke to you, or made you think, that is the Holy "Spirit compelling you to consider Jesus Christ who is revealed on the pages herein. Simply pray the following prayer with intention and sincerity of heart. *"For whosoever shall call upon the name of the Lord shall be saved."* *(Romans 10:13)*

"Dear God,

I know I'm a sinner, and I ask for your forgiveness.

I believe Jesus Christ is Your Son. I believe that He died

for my sin and that you raised Him to life. I want to trust

Him as my Savior and follow Him as Lord from this day

forward. Guide my life and help me to do your will.

I pray this in the name of Jesus. Amen."

Made in the USA
Columbia, SC
21 February 2020